T0147016

TOUSSAINT L'OUVERTURE

This essential new series features classic texts by key figures that took center stage during a period of insurrection. Each book is introduced by a major contemporary radical writer who shows how these incendiary words still have the power to inspire, to provoke and maybe to ignite new revolutions . . .

Also available:

Wu Ming presents Thomas Müntzer:
Sermon to the Princes

Slavoj Žižek presents Trotsky:
Terrorism and Communism

Michael Hardt presents Thomas Jefferson:
The Declaration of Independence

Slavoj Žižek presents Mao:
On Practice and Contradiction

Walden Bello Presents Ho Chi Minh:
Down With Colonialism!

Alain Badiou presents Marx:
The Civil War in France

Tariq Ali presents Castro:
The Declarations of Havana

Slavoj Žižek presents Robespierre:
Virtue and Terror

Terry Eagleton presents Jesus Christ:
The Gospels

Geoffrey Robertson presents The Levellers:
The Putney Debates

TOUSSAINT L'OUVERTURE

THE HAITIAN REVOLUTION

INTRODUCTION BY DR JEAN-BERTRAND ARISTIDE

EDITED BY

NICK NESBITT

VERSO

London • New York

First published by Verso 2008
Introduction © Jean-Bertrand Aristide
© in the selection and editorial matter Verso 2008
All rights reserved

1 3 5 7 9 10 8 6 4 2

Verso
UK: 6 Meard Street, London W1F 0EG
USA: 20 Jay Street, Suite 1010, Brooklyn, NY 11201-8346
www.versobooks.com

Verso is the imprint of New Left Books

ISBN-13: 978-1-84467-261-5

British Library Cataloguing in Publication Data
A catalogue record for this book is available from the British Library

Library of Congress Cataloging-in-Publication Data
A catalog record for this book is available from the Library of Congress

Typeset by Hewer Text UK Ltd, Edinburgh
Printed in the USA

CONTENTS

INTRODUCTION

Dr Jean-Bertrand Aristide

In 1804 Haiti emerged as the first black republic from the world's only successful slave revolution. The outstanding leader who charted the course of this historic event was a slave whose name is now a timeless symbol of freedom: Toussaint L'Ouverture. The written works he left, his memoirs and letters, and the constitution he drafted, offer insight into his political, theological and economic legacy. For us, following in Toussaint's footsteps, his written record raises three core questions. To what extent did Toussaint liberate himself not only from physical slavery, but from mental slavery to the colonial system he fought? Second, on the theological plane, does Toussaint's legacy offer a line of liberation that can be implemented today? And lastly, would fulfilling Toussaint's social and economic legacy allow us to eradicate poverty, the modern version of slavery, and move towards real freedom?

From the transatlantic slave trade to today's global system of economic slavery, broad ranges of players have worked to maintain colonialism. Those I would call mental slaves, the colonized who nonetheless defend the interests of white colonizers, have always played a crucial role in upholding slavery, then and now. Perhaps the most powerful criticism that has been levelled at Toussaint was that he was overprotective of the masters and their system. Loved by a majority, feared by a minority, and perceived by some in hindsight as having been too kind, too gentle and too diplomatic towards the colonizers, Toussaint's true personality emerges in his writings and his achievements. Hence our first question: Did this former slave remain a mental slave to the system he sought to overthrow?

The name of God has been used strategically over four centuries to try to justify slavery. Yet academic discourse on slavery tends to focus much more on the political than the theological dimensions of the slave system. The religious references in Toussaint's writings offer an opportunity to examine this theological field and to question whether Toussaint himself left behind a theological legacy of liberation that can be contextualized or implemented.

The dream held by Toussaint was a two-sided coin: on one side political freedom, on the other economic freedom. Over the past 200 years, very little has been said about Toussaint's determination to eradicate poverty, which was, and still is, inextricably linked to slavery. Thus a third question arises: How can we eradicate poverty by fulfilling Toussaint's social legacy?

TOUSSAINT: FORMER SLAVE NOT MENTAL SLAVE

The nervous system of the human body can be disrupted by both intrinsic and extrinsic disorders. The body politic is susceptible to the same disruptions. Since 1492, and continuing to this day, colonialism and neocolonialism have been a permanent source of extrinsic disorder to Haiti. Internally, mental slaves from the Haitian elite have generated intrinsic pathologies throughout the country's social fabric that have blocked sustainable development. For the colonizers, blacks fell into two categories: slave and mental slave. Which of these was Toussaint L'Ouverture?

François Dominique Toussaint L'Ouverture was the son of Gaou-Guinou, an Arada prince born in present-day Benin,

Africa, who was shipped to Haiti as a slave. Gaou-Guinou was baptized and became known as Hypollite. His second marriage was to a woman named Pauline. The two had four daughters and four sons – Jean, Paul, Pierre and Toussaint. The family lived in Haut du Cap, a village near Cap-Haitian, the second city of Haiti. Toussaint was born on the Bréda Plantation in Cap-Haitian, which in 1786 would become the property of the Comte de Noé. The uncertainty surrounding Toussaint's date of birth reflects how slaves were reduced to objects in the eyes of the colonizers. At least four different dates have been proposed: 1739, based on a letter Toussaint addressed to the French Directory in 1797; 1746, according to his son Isaac; 1743, based on several sources; and 1745, based on documents from Fort de Joux, the French military installation where he was imprisoned, and ultimately died.

At the time of his birth, whatever the date, few thought that he would survive. His frail physique inspired the nickname *Fatra baton*, meaning a stick so thin that it should be thrown in the garbage. But the child surprised everyone. Toussaint developed exceptional physical and intellectual capacities; very early he distinguished himself from the many others on the Bréda Plantation. 'At first assigned to work with the estate animals, L'Ouverture became coachman to the estate manager and then steward of all the livestock.'[1] In 1799, the plantation owner, Bayon de Libertat, said of Toussaint: 'I entrusted to him the principal branch of my management, and the care of the live-stock. Never was my confidence in him disappointed.'

Toussaint had long nurtured good relations with some colonizers, and on the eve of the slave insurrection of 1791 he had even saved some of their lives. His legacy has endured some harsh criticism on this point. But his was essentially a moderate, temperate character, self-controlled and diplomatic in style. Despite the violence of the slave system, Toussaint did not adopt a violent comportment, based in turn on revenge and hatred.

How did he manage to cultivate these precious personal qualities while developing skills vital to navigating within the complex political arena in which he found himself?

The watershed moment for Toussaint took shape sometime in 1790 or 1791, perhaps under the glow of the 14 August 1791 ceremony at Bois Caïman. Toussaint himself was already free; nevertheless he opted to stand with the masses, those who had been reduced to the property of their masters. Toussaint could not fully enjoy his own liberty; he shared the suffering of those who were still victims of slavery. For him to be fully free – and to feel fully free – *all* enslaved persons had to be free.

A year earlier, in 1790, Toussaint had chosen not to join the mobilizing efforts of Vincent Ogé, a free coloured man whose vision of freedom was limited only to his own caste of wealthy and free coloureds, and did not extend to the slaves. Colonial France was 'the first empire to have a democratic imperial policy that included slaves and free coloured . . . That policy did not last very long . . . But it lasted longer in the Caribbean, both before and after it was imperial policy.'[2] Toussaint's vision of liberty was universal at a time when France sought to exploit the divisions (real and created) between the coloured and slave communities.

From August 1791 until his kidnapping by French forces in 1802, Toussaint was propelled into the public arena by this vision of universal liberty. Toussaint understood humanistic needs, or as James Bugental[3] would come to describe it almost 200 years later, the postulates of humanistic psychology:

1. Human beings cannot be reduced to components.
2. Human beings have in them a uniquely human context.
3. Human consciousness includes an awareness of oneself in the context of other people.
4. Human beings have choices and non-desired responsibilities.
5. Human beings are intentional; they seek meaning, value and creativity.

This description of existential human qualities inherently carries within it the seeds of liberty, equality and fraternity.

The slave rebellion that erupted in northern Haiti in the wake of the Bois Caïman ceremony in August 1791 occurred in a region that 'was the earliest densely settled and earliest devoted to sugar, largely because its agricultural plain could support rain-fed sugar cultivation . . . The northern region produced roughly two-fifths of the sugar of Haiti by the beginning of the Revolution, a bit less tonnage than, but equal in value to, that of the western region.'[4] This rebellion ignited an insurrection that was a clear and deep expression of a collective call for freedom. Though he was not an instigator of the rebellion, Toussaint followed the will and interests of the slaves, and in late 1791, just one year after refusing to align with Ogé, Toussaint stepped onto the public stage and responded to the historic call of the slaves. The insurrection needed his leadership, and he created an *ouverture* (opening) towards freedom. Indeed, he was 'L'Ouverture' (The Opening). St-Domingue thus became, in the words of Aimé Césaire, 'the first country in modern times to have posed in reality, and to also have posed for human reflection, the great problem that the twentieth century has not yet succeeded in resolving in all its social, economic, and racial complexity: the colonial problem'.[5]

At the start of the revolution, with almost half a million enslaved Africans in St-Domingue (100,000 new slaves had arrived in just the three preceding years), the colonizers thought they could resolve the colonial problem by exponentially increasing the number of slaves.

The vision of the rebel slaves, of course, was radically different: to eradicate the colonial problem the slaves began by burning down the plantations – the engine of the slave system – and by courageously fighting the colonial masters. Toussaint's approach was less radical. His first choice included neither fire nor the rejection of all whites. When he realized that his former master's family was in imminent danger, Toussaint took precautions to protect them. This move was characteristic of Toussaint, who, throughout the struggle for freedom, systematically sought alliances that could bring him closer to his goal. For similar strategic reasons, in 1793, during the war between France and Spain, Toussaint joined the Spanish camp, which occupied the eastern two-thirds of the island. Serving as an aide to Georges Biassou, one of the most important insurgent leaders in the northern plains, he quickly rose through the ranks.

Because of his exceptional military talents, his ability to build consensus, train soldiers and find strategic ways to achieve victories, Toussaint was recognized as a great general. His authority in the north was legendary. Meanwhile, the French colonizers were desperate to find a counterweight to his ascension and, at the same time, to repel European forces encroaching on their interests. In addition to the Spanish in the east, a British invasion threatened St-Domingue's coastline. The National Assembly in Paris dispatched Léger-Félicité Sonthonax and Etienne Polverel, two French commissioners, to replace General Etienne Laveaux as governor of the colony. Their mission was to lure rebel slaves from the Spanish with the promise of freedom.

Toussaint saw an opening. However dubious the French offer may have been, he saw the opportunity to strengthen his own strategy by joining the French and abandoning the British and the Spanish, who in any event were stalling on the promise of freedom made to the slaves. On 29 August 1793, the very same day that Sonthonax issued his proclamation abolishing slavery in the north, Toussaint issued his own proclamation: 'I want Liberty and Equality to reign in St-Domingue. I work to bring them into existence. Unite yourselves to us, brothers, and fight with us for the same cause.' With these words, Toussaint 'was positioning himself against Sonthonax as the true defender of liberty in St-Domingue'.[6] He officially aligned himself with the French in 1794, only after the French National Assembly had sanctioned the Sonthonax proclamation against slavery. He then immediately began to pressure the French to put a definitive end to slavery throughout the colony.

Promoted to Général de Brigade by Laveaux, former Governor of St-Domingue, Toussaint led his army of blacks, mulattos and whites and won a number of victories, routing the Spanish from the island.

Meanwhile, in 1794, French forces led by Victor Hugues regained control of the neighbouring island of Guadeloupe from the British, who had briefly occupied it with the support of local plantation owners.[7] This successful restoration of French power in Guadeloupe was a potential threat to Toussaint's plan for the total eradication of slavery in St-Domingue.

> The freedom of planter governments in the colonies means by definition that arbitrary imperial governments do not have the right to interfere with their decisions. The freedom of the planters to do what they want with their property means that slaves do not have freedom, the right to do what they want.[8]

Slavery formed the foundation of the colonial economy: the unpaid labour of slaves was the principal source of riches for the colonizers, and St-Domingue stood at the pinnacle of this wealth:

> [In the 1790s the colony] produced close to one-half of all the sugar and coffee consumed in Europe and the Americas, as well as substantial amounts of cotton, indigo, and ground provisions. Though scarcely larger than Maryland, and little more than twice the size of Jamaica, it had long been the wealthiest colony in the Caribbean and was hailed by publicists as the 'Pearl of the Antilles' or the 'Eden of the Western World.' . . . By 1789 Saint Domingue had about 8,000 plantations producing crops for export. They generated some

two-fifths of France's foreign trade, a proportion rarely equaled in any colonial empire.[9]

It was clear the colonizers would fight tooth-and-nail to keep this source of wealth.

In 1795, Toussaint found himself in a complex strategic position. As he manoeuvred forward, he had to balance ethics and moral values with strategic planning. He was able to revive the economy of St-Domingue while significantly improving social conditions on the island. He believed that social tensions could be reduced by encouraging unity among blacks, coloureds and whites. Although freed from the whip, the former slaves would have to work hard; Toussaint did not tolerate laziness: 'Work', he said, 'is necessary, it is a virtue.' But now the wealth generated by the former slaves would directly benefit them. Unfortunately, this vision did not fit in with colonial plans. Despite economic and social progress made by 1795, the road to freedom was still long. Forever faithful to the masses of slaves, and committed to building alliances to reach his goal, he abandoned whoever thought that he, Toussaint, could be used against his people. In 1797, Toussaint broke ranks with Sonthonax for precisely this reason.

Generally, blacks and mulattos who were of the political, intellectual or economic elite, and who benefited by serving as mental slaves to the colonizers, failed to recognize that the experience of slavery itself 'formed the root of an emergent collective identity through an equally emergent collective memory, one that signified and distinguished a race, a people'.[10] The psychological obsessions and inferiority complexes of internal colonization prevented the colonized from understanding that a transfer of class does not mean a change of self or identity. Such mental slaves, then as now, live in a near permanent state of identity crisis. As feelings of inferiority weaken their sense of identity, they constantly look to the white master with whom they identify – much as Frantz Fanon famously described in his seminal work *Black Skin, White Masks*.[11]

By contrast, hierarchical divisions between enslaved Africans and white colonizers helped raise the slaves' consciousness of their condition. Toussaint knew that the slaves could gain power only through unity, whereas those who remained mentally enslaved were, by definition, powerless. In this respect, Toussaint's perception of power opposed that of Sonthonax. While never forsaking his convictions, Toussaint did have the ability to understand multiple perspectives. He understood that the exercise of power required continuous vigilance and identification of different types of enemies – the immediate enemy and the enemy to come.[12]

At the same time Toussaint showed that he could reach compromises with those who pursued interests broadly compatible with his own. In 1798, Toussaint agreed to negotiate on behalf of France for the withdrawal of British forces from St-Domingue and for greater commercial exchanges with foreign nations. He signed economic agreements with Britain and the United States to sell sugar, coffee and other produce in exchange for needed weapons and foreign manufactured goods. Signed on 22 May 1799, these agreements were a step towards prosperity; they were also a testament to Toussaint's principles and his capacity to think strategically. The two contracting countries offered to recognize Toussaint as king, ruler of an independent nation. Because, as C. L. R. James rightly noted, Toussaint understood that power was a 'means to an end' – in this case, true liberty for all slaves – he refused the offer. He was not obsessed with power for power's sake. Toussaint signed the trade agreements because they could bring something to his people. But he refused to be crowned 'king' by the same white colonizers responsible for the continued enslavement of his people.[13]

In any case, Toussaint did not need to be king. He was loved, even revered, by his people. His view of leadership was expansive; he opened his arms to all – black, mulatto and white

– and this empowered him to achieve much during his administration. The increased agricultural production sparked by Toussaint's policies not only brought needed resources to the country, it was a collective expression of the dignity of the former enslaved Africans turned agricultural workers.

Toussaint's success in reversing the economic prospects of St-Domingue was also a measure of his charisma as a leader. According to Robert C. Solomon,

> Charisma has much to do with emotion, but not just the emotion generated by leaders. It is also, first and foremost, the passion of the leader. It is strange, then, that the nature of emotion, the very heart of charisma, should have been so long neglected by leadership scholars. What has also been neglected, along with emotion, is the intimate relationship between emotion and ethics.[14]

Studies on Toussaint have often focused only on his military prowess and discipline, and not enough on this intimate relationship between love, ethics and leadership.

For Toussaint, power and leadership operated relationally and reciprocally. In this vision of leadership, to control the balance of power a leader must care about the fundamental needs of his or her followers. Toussaint shaped a strategy that consistently demonstrated that he cared deeply for the dignity and prosperity of his people. Signing trade agreements with the British and the Americans while flatly rejecting the offer to be crowned king was one example. Another was his expulsion of his nominal French superior Gabriel Hédouville and of Hédouville's successor Philippe Roume. When Hédouville first arrived from France with the 'difficult mission to reassert metropolitan control in the colony', Toussaint let Hédouville know exactly what he was thinking: 'There are men who talk as if they support general liberty, but who inside are its sworn enemies.'[15]

Toussaint's commitment to universal liberty was not shared by many of his foreign contemporaries. Two years after signing the trade agreement with Toussaint, Thomas Jefferson would begin to undermine it. Given the social and geopolitical complexity of the context in which Toussaint led the enslaved Africans and their descendants, we are compelled to ask how he managed to become such an outstanding liberator. The political participation of the slaves was certainly an indispensable driving force against the enemies. But so too was Toussaint's character, his personality. I refer here to the essence of his person and his self-consciousness.[16] And in his essence he was a free man. Toussaint consistently demonstrated intellectual independence from the colonizers, even while maintaining the ability to negotiate with them when necessary. Time and again, Toussaint demonstrated his own autonomy, his ability to manoeuvre, to lead, and to *shape* events, rather than merely to respond to them. He set his own course, and this the colonizers ultimately found intolerable.

The fundamental interests of blacks and whites in eighteenth-century St-Domingue were poles apart. To manoeuvre in such complex territory, Toussaint often had to change tactics and modify plans, but he was always consistent in his basic principles. He never took one stand while in the company of the master and the opposite stand when among his own people. Duplicity of this kind is characteristic of mental slaves who define themselves in terms of their dependency on their masters. The social dimensions of their selves betray their distance from their social origins. Within their own societies, mental slaves identify themselves as members of the elite. It is inconceivable to them that all people have equal social standing. They internalize and then invert their own psychological subordination.

Anyone who wants to understand the process by which European colonizers succeeded in using the colonized in their indirect rule over the natives they dominated should pay careful attention to the psychological dimensions of colonialism. In this context, the 'self' is an object of inquiry – a crucial site of colonial and anti-colonial struggle.[17] According to William Easterly, in British Nigeria in 1939 there were 1,315 British citizens in charge of 20 million Nigerians, while 2,384 Europeans ruled over 9.4 million Africans in the Belgian Congo and 3,660 Europeans imposed their will on 15 million Africans in French-occupied West Africa.[18] When Toussaint emerged, in 1791, as the great leader of St-Domingue, approximately 40,000 white colonizers there were ruling over 30,000 *machotara*,[19] or coloureds, and 500,000 slaves, two-thirds of whom had been born in Africa. How did the minority manage to control the majority? They certainly could not have succeeded without the help of mental slaves – people who lacked genuine autonomy and a national identity. Discussing the psychology of national identity and nationalism, Karl E. Scheibe notes that, despite the potential dangers inherent in the concept of nationalism, national identity 'has been the principle force at work in the massive postwar trend toward the decolonization of territories formerly dominated by European powers'.[20]

> If there is something at the heart of identity formation, and if that something has common elements among all people, then there is the basis for understanding and possibly resolving political conflicts over identity. If, in contrast, identities are somehow exclusive and inherent to the makeup of the individual, then politics must be concerned with irreducible differences and the conflicts that go with them.[21]

Slavery and its attendant economic exploitation were permanent sources of political conflict in the colony. But the issue of identity occupied an important space, because the contours of identity traced by the elite and the mental slave were exclusive: the elites were human, slaves were not. Kenneth Hoover confirms that 'what identity analysis demonstrates is that, independently of economic advantage or disadvantage, considerations of identity have the potential both to tear communities apart and bring them together'.[22]

This legacy is with us still. More than 200 years later, Haitian identity is still split, with the great mass of the Haitian people on one side, and a small elite who remain identified with today's colonizers on the other. In 2004, Toussaint's descendants experienced the destructive powers of this split. White neocolonial forces, allied with today's Haitian mental slaves, vowed to use violence to disrupt and prevent the bicentennial commemoration of the very events around which Haitian mass national identity was formed:

1. Toussaint's constitution proclaiming freedom for all in 1801;
2. Toussaint's assassination in Fort de Joux on 7 April 1803;
3. The birth of Haiti's flag, symbolizing a radical rejection of French colonialism, on 18 May 1803;
4. The last battle of Vertières, marking the historic victory of enslaved Haitians over the then superpower of the world, Napoleon's army, on 18 November 1803;
5. The independence of the world's first black republic, Haiti, on 1 January 1804.

Neocolonizers spent more than US$200 million dollars to ensure that the descendants of Toussaint would not be able to celebrate these historic events. But the masses of the Haitian people, whose identity stems from them, commemorated the Revolution anyway. With courage and pride, representatives of the youngest black republic, South Africa, joined with the oldest black republic on 1 January 2004 in Haiti to honour common African ancestors and celebrate the universal value of freedom. South African President Thabo Mbeki, his wife Zanele, the Minister of Foreign Affairs Dr N. Zuma, and the rest of a prestigious South African delegation received an *ubuntu*[23] welcome from 8 million

Haitian descendants of Africa. Although time is a limited commodity for a head of state, President Mbeki has found time to research Toussaint L'Ouverture and analyze his achievements. He writes:

More than 200 years ago, in 1802, Haiti was in the grip of an intense military and political struggle that was waged by African slaves, to liberate themselves from French slave owners, and from French domination. Angered by the sustained struggle of the slaves, Napoleon said: 'Toussaint . . . this gilded African . . . I will not rest until I have torn the epaulettes off every nigger in the colonies . . . Toussaint L'Ouverture has chosen a course of action which is quite impossible and which the Metropole considers most intolerable. At this time, they don't even wish to discuss the matter further, these black leaders, these ungrateful and rebellious Africans.' However neither Napoleon nor the French armies commanded among others by his brother-in-law, General Leclerc, could tear the epaulettes off the 'ungrateful and rebellious Africans'. The struggle in Haiti culminated in the proclamation on 1 January 1804 of Haiti as the first ever independent Black Republic.[24]

Our 2004 Bicentennial offered Haitians a unique opportunity to celebrate unity and common identity with the descendants of Africa: a delegation from Toussaint's ancestral home of Benin; the African diaspora, represented by the prime minister of the Bahamas, Perry Christy, US Congresswoman Maxine Waters, her husband Ambassador Williams and Mme Hazel Robinson, among others, who paid tribute to Toussaint's memory and achievements. African–American scholar and activist Molefi Kete Asante wrote eloquently: 'There was no other place for me to be on January 1, 2004 but in Haiti . . . one of the most potent symbols of black revolution against injustice in the annals of history.'[25] That indescribable day, marked by the heroic presence of representatives of the vast African family, is forever imprinted in the collective memory of the Haitian people. Such deep solidarity and profound communion is captured by the exceptional writer and social justice activist, Randall Robinson, who wrote in his most recent book, *An Unbroken Agony*:

> It is not overstating to suggest that across the globe the Haitian revolutionaries with their magnificent victory had, to paraphrase Martinican writer Frantz Fanon, 'set afoot' a *new* black woman, man, child . . . The days of involuntary servitude were, at long last, numbered. Most everyone everywhere – enslaved and enslaver alike – recognized that the countdown to slavery's end had been set ticking by the Haitian Toussaint L'Ouverture, and his triumphant army of ex-slaves.[26]

Why, then, outside the African diaspora, was the commemoration of the world's only successful slave revolution so little noted? Since the moment the enslaved Africans of Haiti rose up, colonialists and neocolonialists have used every means at their disposal, notably the pens of historians, to keep the world from knowing the truth of the Haitian Revolution, and specifically of how French colonizers kidnapped Toussaint, assassinated his character and then killed him in Fort de Joux.

The mental slaves who continue to serve the colonial order have never had the moral courage to challenge this manipulation. Rather than confront Napoleon's crimes against Toussaint and the Haitian people, they choose actively to promote historical amnesia. Mythomaniacal colonizers and the mental slaves who mimic them share a pathological proclivity towards lying. Together they reinforce the sclerosis of the colonial and neocolonial system. It is not surprising then that neocolonizers recruit mental slaves as they prepare to re-enter the political scene of a former colony.

Both the first coup d'état against Toussaint's successor on 17 October 1806 and the most recent coup in Haiti, on 29 February 2004, illustrate the barbarity that will be used to overthrow any head of state who is neither a mental slave nor a corrupt dictator defending the interests of the wealthy and their foreign masters. In 2004 the neocolonizers demonstrated once again that, for them, a Haitian president must be both a puppet and a mental slave. Unfortunately, they have so far succeeded.

But the Haitian people have achieved a high level of consciousness, and, like Toussaint, they will never give up. To the pertinent question posed by Jean Twenge and Roy Baumeister, 'How do people react to social exclusion and rejection?',[27] The people of Haiti answer simply but profoundly: 'We follow Toussaint L'Ouverture.'

TOUSSAINT'S THEOLOGICAL LEGACY IN CONTEXT

Toussaint's colonial detractors accused him of using the Catholic religion as a cover for the secret worship of Vaudou spirits. Even his name, 'L'Ouverture', was said to reference a *lwa* (African spirit) called *Legba* – the one who opens the gates. The designation of Catholicism as Haiti's sole official religion in Toussaint's Constitution of 1801 and his continued devotion to the Roman Catholic Church were claimed to be part of the ruse. From this point of view, Toussaint was not a 'true' Christian.

From other quarters it is Toussaint's embrace of Catholicism that has been criticized. Slavery was imposed in the name of God. Is this the same God who was at the centre of Toussaint's faith? In 1492 Christopher Columbus declared that the enslaved Africans were savages in need of civilizing, and presented them with the cross of Jesus Christ. How could Toussaint confess his faith in *that* cross *and* fiercely oppose slavery? From the point of view of liberation theology, the question we might pose is: Between

Toussaint and Columbus, who was the true follower of Jesus, the Liberator par excellence?

While it would not be accurate to call Toussaint a 'liberation theologist', looking at his legacy and his relationship to Christianity through the lens of liberation theology can be helpful. What is the theology of liberation, and what do we mean when we speak of a 'preferential option for the poor'? Twenty-five years ago my students would ask: 'Does the option for the poor mean an option against the rich?' I always answered with a resounding no. The option for the poor is preferential, not exclusive. There is resonance here with Toussaint's impulse, throughout his life, and notably in the constitution he drafted, to put the slaves first, but to include all.

Liberation theology finds in the Bible a flat rejection of the exclusion of the poor. Jesus answered John the Baptist, 'Go and tell John that the good news is preached to the poor' (Matt. 11:5). Henceforth all were compelled to demonstrate a commitment to implementing God's directive: 'You will love your neighbour the way you love yourself' (Lev. 19:18 – וְאָהַבְתָּ לְרֵעֲךָ כָּמוֹךָ). From this it follows that, if you do not want to be a slave, you must not enslave your neighbour. These words from the gospel contain the seeds for the emergence of a new society, in which human relationships are rooted in respect, equality and dignity – a way forward from slavery to freedom, from social exclusion to inclusion.

Today, as many as two-thirds of the world's population are marginalized because of their social condition: every day 800 million people are victims of starvation; nearly 11 million children die before their fifth birthday; in 2001, 1.1 billion people subsisted on less than $1 a day, and 2.7 billion on less than $2 a day; only 15 per cent of people infected by HIV/Aids can afford antiretroviral drugs, and more than 3 million people therefore die from the pandemic, one-third of whom live in sub-Saharan Africa. Day after day the poor are becoming poorer. In a clear rupture with the pattern over previous decades, global inequality has increased sharply since the 1980s, while global economic integration has grown. This expansion of extreme poverty coincides with an explosion of wealth.[28] From an economic point of view, Haiti remains the poorest country in the Western hemisphere. Today the poor still bear the cross of marginalization, racism and misery.

Without doubt, the historic causes of ongoing poverty and social stigmatization are rooted in colonialism, slavery and globalization. And in all of this Christianity has colluded. Harvey Sindima writes that 'in colonial Africa, the missionary hegemony worked hand in hand with the colonial powers'.[29] However, Sindima also recognizes that

> in its humble beginnings Christianity was the religion of the poor for it gave them hope . . . As one looks at what is happening in Africa several questions arise: What happened to the revolutionary message, the idea of being on the side of the poor, those made hopeless by the powerful?[30]

This same dichotomy was at work in Toussaint's life. While Christianity was used to justify slavery, ironically Jesuit missionary priests, among others, played an important role in helping Toussaint to articulate his Christian faith and his political option for the slaves.[31] These religious influences should not be underestimated.

As we know, 1 billion Africans and descendants of Africa were caught up in the transatlantic slave trade. It spanned three continents and endured for more than four centuries. Throughout, God was used by the master against the slave, as is illustrated in this story:

> In their hunt for African slaves to send to America, a group of colonizers and their allies kidnapped a family. They set fire to the house but the father managed to escape. The colonizers threatened to burn the wife and the children. The slave master

ordered the eldest son to accompany his colonial collaborators on their search for the escaped man. They slung the innocent young man across the back of a horse and, *Ab hoc et ab hac*, '*A tort et à travers*', began to look, high and low, for him. After hours of searching in vain the colonizers returned and reported that the son refused to disclose the whereabouts of his father. Looking at him still slung across the back of the horse, the furious master asked: Where is your father who is now my slave? Show me where he is or I will immediately burn you in that fire. Are you for me, your master, or for the slave? The suffering youth was unable to answer. Incensed, the master said to his collaborators: Put him aside to be burnt. He called forward one of the escaped slave's daughters and asked: Are you for me, your master, or for my slave who dared to run away? Yes, replied the girl, I am for my father. This answer pleased the colonist. Excellent! You will not be burnt, he exclaimed: '*God is my father. If you are for him, then you are for me.*'

The image of God, often manipulated to justify what cannot be justified, became 'a necessary being'.[32] Carl Gustav Jung associated the God-image with the power of imagination.[33] Modern psychology, particularly analytical psychology, is not content simply to point out the various psychic elements contained in religion, but also examines the function of religion in the individual's personality, what place it has in the human psyche as a whole.[34] There is no doubt that this image of God supporting the master over the slave persists in this era of globalization. 'The religious behaviour of man is intricately related to his other behaviour, economic, familial, and political. Religion does not exist in isolation, nor does man's religious behaviour occur in social isolation.'[35]

The interrelationship between economic and religious power during the transatlantic slave trade can be illuminated by the philosophy of religion, which embraces religion as an inherent and necessary feature of human consciousness. It also assumes knowledge of God. Religion thereby becomes a branch of philosophy as a whole. Hegel's explanations of that topic remain profoundly relevant.[36]

If, on one hand, philosophy of religion addresses the issue of ethics, on the other hand sociology of religion looks at the interrelationships among groups, states, and religious organizations, focusing on the motivation of their ideologies.[37] From colonialism to neocolonialism, we must look for the unspoken message that underpins official religious statements. In the post-colonial era some religions have continued to be used as an important ideological tool in keeping the poor politically passive, the objects rather than the subjects of their own history. Frequently, religious pronouncements pretend to draw a moral or ethical line, while paradoxically, the unspoken – and real – message is devoid of any moral principle. When it is necessary to lie, they lie. And a lie is best covered with another lie. *The Uses of Haiti*, one of the most compelling of several books written by Dr Paul Farmer, aptly demonstrates these tactics in the Haitian context.

The underlying impetus of the colonial project is succinctly summed up in this Latin expression: *Auri sacra fame!* ('the dreadful and avaricious search for gold'). The fundamental motivation is bound to the economic interest of the master and/or the system that he represents. From this philosophical perspective the master (or the system) links the concept of 'faith' to economic interest. Faith in money first, faith in God if it is expedient – for instance, if that God justifies all the means used to increase the master's wealth. Otherwise, we must consider religion and philosophy as refusals of faith. In that regard, says Ronald Hall, 'religion in general, and Christianity in particular, can be, and often are, at odds with faith'.[38]

In this paradigm there is no place for the prophetic voice. John the Baptist, Jesus, Toussaint, and more recently Nelson Mandela, were condemned, each in turn, for defending the victims of injustice rather than supporting the interests of the master.

When, in the 1970s and 1980s, this prophetic voice was heard across Latin America, when the proponents of liberation theology, the bishops and priests and the poor themselves, began to promote social peace emerging from the gospel of love, they too were condemned.

In 1802, after promulgating the Haitian Constitution, which recognized the slaves as human beings and declared the liberty of all black people, Toussaint L'Ouverture, in the eyes of the masters, deserved death. He was kidnapped and taken to France, where he died in jail on 7 April 1803. But his death did not end the struggle in Haiti. That same year, the slaves of Haiti – both those born in the country and in Africa – won the final battle against Napoleon's army, defeating the world's greatest superpower, and securing their independence.

We believe, as I have said, that the option for the slaves or for the poor is preferential, not exclusive. When the quality of life for the poor improves, the rich also benefit. Abject poverty and social peace are diametrically opposed to one another. There must be investment in human development to guarantee social cohesion. Gustavo Gutiérrez said that Christianity is the way by which the Spirit leads the new 'messianic people', the church, through history. This historic journey is a collective one because an entire community accomplishes it.[39] By the same token, wherever one person is oppressed the entire community is affected.

Preaching the message of Jesus is an important step; but, in reality, it is not the definitive one. The ultimate act undertaken by those willing to reach the pinnacle of love for the poor is to be in deep communion and communication within the community of faith. This communion with his people characterized Toussaint's leadership. 'Brothers and Friends,' he proclaimed, 'I want liberty and equality to reign in St-Domingue. I am working to make that happen. Unite yourselves to us, brothers, and fight with us for the same cause.' While Columbus enslaved in the name of God, Toussaint freed in the name of love, which for us is another name for God. This is Toussaint's theological legacy.

TOUSSAINT'S SOCIAL LEGACY IN CONTEXT

The vital question before us is how to cut the chains of misery that still bind the hands of Toussaint's descendants, and of those worldwide trapped in poverty. Toussaint's fierce opposition to slavery, his leadership skills, his freedom-inspired writings and the constitution he drafted bequeath to us all a strategy for opposing injustice. When Toussaint struggled to increase production to feed the people of St-Domingue and raise the country's export levels, everyone was required to respect the discipline and strict measures imposed by the Constitution of 1801. This example tells us that discipline is part of the equation.

More than 200 years after Toussaint's kidnapping, Haiti, the world's first independent black republic, remains in abject poverty. Although, according to Michael Lipton, 'knowledge about poverty has increased more in the past four decades than in the previous two millennia',[40] we still have many unanswered questions. 'Few questions', said Mark Robert Rank, 'have generated as much discussion across time as those pertaining to the causes of human impoverishment.'[41]

Poverty is deeply rooted in colonialism, neoliberalism and globalization (which implies neocolonialism). The colonial project and those who led it prioritized financial capital over human capital; centuries later, neocolonialists remain motivated by this same interest. For the most part, this motivation reflects an obsession whose roots extend back to the transatlantic slave trade, a crime against humanity of immense magnitude and incomparable suffering. Institutionalized racism became embedded in Western society; it generated social pathologies and created schizophrenic economies in the colonies where slavery flourished. To conceal their real motivations, colonizers depicted the slaves as barbarous, uncivilized and inferior. Adam Smith, father of capitalism, wrote that

> the interest which occasioned the first settlement of the different European colonies in America and the West Indies was not altogether so plain and distinct as that which directed the establishment of those of ancient Greece and Rome . . . The colonies, in the times preceding the foundation of Rome, were inhabited by barbarous and uncivilized nations.[42]

In order to win the economic war, lies were readily deployed as weapons of mass destruction. These enduring historical falsifications and discriminatory portrayals have enduring pathological consequences for the victims of this psychological war. And once the virus of inferiority implants itself in the collective psyche, it takes a long time to uproot.

Predictably, colonization brought genocide and abject poverty to Haiti's first inhabitants; and the African slaves introduced to replace them were compelled to work like animals. The blood of Africans and the labour of Toussaint's people caused the colony of St-Domingue to flourish economically, and it became the richest of the French colonies. The country produced 60 per cent of the world's coffee, and at one point its exports exceeded the combined production of the thirteen colonies of the future United States. The livelihood of one out of every eight French citizens depended on the slave economy of St-Domingue. This paradox reflected the social disorder and social pathologies rampant in the country. Maurice Parmelee would describe these as 'abnormal social phenomena, which impede or are supposed to impede the course of social evolution'.[43] These 'abnormal and pathological mental phenomena [led] to poverty and its attendant evils', affirms Parmelee.[44] Other scholars, such as John Read, argue that being poor, or being a member of a colonized people, can have psychological consequences. Poverty and racism can be identified as causative factors for psychosis.[45]

When the wounds of poverty are so deep, so far-reaching and so historically rooted, how then can we begin to heal them? It is in this light that we should look at the broad issues of reparation and restitution, which hold within them the possibility not only for economic repair, but also for the psychic repair of the wounds of colonialism and its legacy of poverty. In the case of Haiti, in 1825, after defeating Napoleon's army, the new nation was forced to pay France 90 million francs. The present value of this amount, which generations of Haitians laboured to pay, is US$21 billion. It is hard to imagine a more onerous 'debt'. In 2004, the government of Haiti raised the issue of the restitution of this 'debt' by France before the world. Many commentators have pointed to this call for restitution as one of the prime motivations for the neocolonial coup of 29 February 2004.

And yet we maintain that, for any society to call itself civilized, it must be ready to address this issue of restitution and reparations within a framework of mutual respect. Just as Toussaint could not predict how long it would take to end slavery, we cannot know how long it will take to end poverty, or when restitution will come. But certainly we can and must accelerate this process by focusing on the following steps:

1. We must struggle against economic and psychological enslavement, draw upon African values, and look to the findings of the United Nations World Conference Against Racism, hosted in Durban in 2001.
2. We must promote the globalization of human solidarity, and not the globalization of the economy. This option implies both human growth and economic growth.

3. We must resist neoliberalism and savage privatizations. They engender schizophrenic economies that in turn reinforce structural corruption at local and international levels, and contribute to weakening the state in its fight against poverty.

4. We must give the poor access to micro-credit.

5. We must promote social cohesion through democratic and economic partnership between the private and public sectors. Classical liberalism conceives of the social and economic arena as a place of 'free' competition between self-interested individuals, unfettered by regulations or public values. But recent history shows that the attempt to impose such 'freedoms' through structural adjustment programmes and policies targeting macroeconomic stabilization – the favoured strategies of neoliberalism – actually generates unending conflict.[46]

6. We must work for democratic principles, good governance, and respect for human rights, all of which constitute an indispensable environment for promoting both human growth and economic growth.

7. We must reject neoliberalism and instead invest in human beings: education, literacy, school lunch programmes, free schooling; healthcare in which people have access to drugs for HIV/Aids, tuberculosis and malaria; and access to clean water and sanitation.

8. We must call on all states to respect their commitments to implement the United Nations Millennium Declaration, signed in September 2000.

9. We must respect the rights of women and men equally, which means that women too must have access to land. Undertaken within a legal framework, agrarian reform or land redistribution can contribute to the ending of social tensions. In the struggle against poverty, land represents one of the most important assets.

10. We must approach debt cancellation in the light of this Hebrew proverb: .אל ׳ סתכל בקנקן, אלא במה שבתוכו ('Don't look at the jar, but at what's inside it').

On this last point, the history of Haiti's debt is an example of the duplicitous role that foreign aid can play in economically burdening a nation.[47] Peace activist Tom Ricker, of the Quixote Center in the United States, sketched out the path of Haiti's recent debt obligations:

Of the roughly $600 million that Haiti supposedly owes the InterAmerican Development Bank, only 43 per cent was actually disbursed to an elected government . . . Roughly half of Haiti's current debt burden – from all sources – was accrued before the 1990 elections . . . The World Bank approved $37 million in new loans to the Aristide government; $30 million of this was approved 6 days before the coup . . . The same World Bank had distributed $256 million in loans to the government of Jean-Claude Duvalier [and] another $158 million to the series of military rulers that governed Haiti between Duvalier's departure in February of 1986, and Aristide's election . . . The IDB did little better, approving a paltry $12 million in loans to the new democracy in Haiti during its short-lived 7 months . . . After approving $110 million in loans to the military junta that ruled Haiti prior to the elections, including $55 million in 1990 alone [and] withholding millions in assistance to an elected government, the IDB approved $200 million in new loans in November of 2003 – most of which would not be disbursed until *after* the coup in February of 2004.[48]

With this history in mind, can there be any doubt that debt cancellation is both vital to Haiti's struggle to eradicate poverty, and morally justified?

However poor Haiti is from an economic standpoint, in culture, history and struggle we are rich, and continue to surprise the world. Our culture and history nurture the resilience of the population, so much so that, despite our material poverty, suicide is almost unheard of.

As a descendant of Africa, Toussaint was nourished by African values. Haitians today continue to draw psychological strength from cultural values deeply rooted in *ubuntu*. *Ubuntu ngumuntu ngabantu* ('a person is a person through other people'). *Ubuntu* generates a collective ego and a social love that crystallizes in brotherhood. These are the seeds for developing a culture of global solidarity. In a clear expression of that solidarity, the 2.5 million Haitians living abroad sent more than US$1.65 billion to relatives at home in 2006. This amount represents twice Haiti's national budget, and 30 per cent of its gross domestic product. In fact, if you add the approximately US$400 million in food and goods that Haitians send home through the informal sector, total remittances are estimated at more than US$2 billion annually. Beyond their economic impact in the struggle against poverty, remittances symbolize an unbreakable chain of solidarity among the descendants of Africa. The spirit of *ubuntu* nurtures and enriches cultures far beyond the geographical borders of Africa.

In the words of our African proverb, we affirm: *Itemba alibulali*[49] – hope is not dead! Toussaint nourished hope in his heart to the end. In 1802, even as he was being led away by his kidnappers, he saw Haiti's independence on the horizon, though it was still invisible, unthinkable to the colonizers:

> In overthrowing me, you have cut only the trunk of the tree of liberty.
> It will spring up again for its roots are numerous and deep!

Pretoria, South Africa – April 2008

SUGGESTED FURTHER READING

Barthélemy, Gérard, *L'Univers rural Haïtien: Le pays en dehors* (Harmattan, 1990).

Bell, Madison Smartt, *All Souls' Rising* (Vintage, 1995).

——————*Toussaint Louverture: A Biography* (Pantheon Books, 2007).

Blackburn, Robin, *The Overthrow of Colonial Slavery: 1776–1848* (Verso, 1988).

Dubois, Laurent, *Avengers of the New World: The Story of the Haitian Revolution* (Harvard University Press, 2004).

Dubois, Laurent and John D. Garrigus, eds, *Slave Revolution in the Caribbean 1789–1804: A Brief History with Documents* (Bedford St Martin's, 2006).

Fick, Carolyn, *The Making of Haiti: The Saint-Domingue Revolution From Below* (University of Tennessee Press, 1990).

Fischer, Sibylle, *Modernity Disavowed: Haiti and the Cultures of Slavery in the Age of Revolution* (Duke University Press, 2004).

Geggus, David, *Haitian Revolutionary Studies* (Indiana University Press, 2002).

——————'Toussaint Louverture and the Haitian Revolution', in R. William Weisberger, ed., *Profiles of Revolutionaries in Atlantic History, 1750–1850* (Columbia University Press, 2007), pp. 115–35.

Hallward, Peter, *Damming the Flood: Haiti, Aristide, and the Politics of Containment* (Verso, 2008).

James, C. L. R., *The Black Jacobins: Toussaint L'Ouverture and the San Domingo Revolution* (Vintage, 1989).

Laurent, Gérard M., *Toussaint Louverture à travers sa correspondance (1794–1798)* (Industrias Gráficas España, 1953).

Nesbitt, Nick, *Universal Emancipation: The Haitian Revolution and the Radical Enlightenment* (University of Virginia Press, 2008).

Pluchon, Pierre, *Toussaint Louverture: Un révolutionnaire noir d'Ancien Régime* (Fayard, 1989).

Popkin, Jeremy, *Facing Racial Revolution: Eyewitness Accounts of the Haitian Insurrection* (University of Chicago Press, 2008).

Scott, David, *Conscripts of Modernity: The Tragedy of Colonial Enlightenment* (Duke University Press, 2004).

Trouillot, Michel-Rolph, *Silencing the Past: Power and the Production of History* (Beacon, 1995).

————*Haiti: State Against Nation: The Origins and Legacy of Duvalierism* (Monthly Review Press, 1990).

CHRONOLOGY

1739–46(?)	Toussaint Bréda, grandson of the Arada African king Gaou-Guinou, born on the Habitation Bréda plantation in the French sugar colony of St-Domingue. Receives a rudimentary education, eventually becoming an expert horse trainer, veterinarian, healer, steward's coachman, and principal manager of the livestock on the plantation.
1776	Toussaint Bréda granted freedom from slavery. Toussaint remains on the Habitation Bréda under the beneficent direction of his former owner, Bayon de Libertat, while purchasing plantations and at least thirteen slaves of his own.
1782	Toussaint marries Suzanne Simon Baptiste.
1791 15 May:	French Assembly grants full political rights to mixed-race citizens.
August:	Slave leaders meet in Bois Caïman to plan rebellion. Night of August 22–23, Haitian Revolution begins under leaders Boukman and Jeannot.
24 September:	Repeal of May 15 law, driving mixed-race citizens to join slave rebellion.

1791–93	Toussaint plays a fundamental, behind-the-scenes role in fomenting and radicalizing the St-Domingue slave rebellion.

1792
April: Assembly again grants political rights to mixed-race and free black citizens of St-Domingue.

1793
February: France declares war against Spain.
June: Toussaint leads rebels fighting the French, repeatedly defeating French forces numerically far superior to his own 600 men. Toussaint controls Northeast St-Domingue, from Marmelade to Dondon.

August: Commissioner Sonthonax unilaterally abolishes slavery, immediately and universally, in St-Domingue. Toussaint Bréda simultaneously issues a call to arms for 'Liberty and Equality', adopting the name Toussaint L'Ouverture and taking his place at the forefront of the movement to overthrow slavery in St-Domingue. Toussaint will continue to fight on the side of the Spanish until spring 1794, by which time he is certain the French Assembly has formally abolished slavery.

1794
March: Toussaint ambushed by rival rebels Jean-François and/or Biassou; he narrowly escapes, but his brother Pierre is killed.

May: Toussaint joins the French republican forces. Under General Laveaux, Toussaint's 4,000 troops quickly secure St-Domingue's Western Belt from Gonaïves to Dondon, defeating all Spanish troops in the region.

June: Abolition of slavery by the French Convention (16 Pluviôse/February 4) officially decreed in St-Domingue.
July: Toussaint defeats the rebel leader Jean-François, still siding with the Spanish.

September –October:	Toussaint unsuccessfully fights troops of British Lieutenant Colonel Brisbane for control of St Marc.
1794–98	Toussaint maintains a voluminous correspondence with his principal protector and benefactor, General Etienne Laveaux.
1795 July:	Treaty of Basel ends war between France and Spain, Spain ceding eastern Hispaniola (present-day Dominican Republic) to France. Toussaint promoted to brigadier general.
August:	Thermidorian Constitution reaffirms abolition of slavery.
October:	Napoleon Bonaparte made Commander-in-Chief of French Army.
November:	Jean-François and Biassou abandon Hispaniola.
1796 March:	Amid growing conflict between mixed-race and black troops, Laveaux is captured at Cap Français by colored officials, then freed by troops under Toussaint's delegate Pierre Michel.
April:	Laveaux proclaims Toussaint the 'black Spartacus, the negro [who] Raynal predicted would avenge the outrages done to his race'. Toussaint is promoted to lieutenant governor.
July:	Commissioner Sonthonax promotes Toussaint to general of division. Toussaint is now the most powerful commander in St-Domingue, controlling the entire Northern Department of the colony.
October:	At Toussaint's insistence, Laveaux returns to France as colonial representative to defend the cause of emancipation in an increasingly reactionary political atmosphere.
1797	Toussaint acts to instate paid plantation labour, encountering widespread resistance from former

	slaves. Conflict develops between Toussaint and Sonthonax over Toussaint's desire to restore property to white plantation owners who condemn slavery.
April:	L'Ouverture recaptures Mirebelais from the British. A royalist majority is elected to the National Assembly. Representative Vincent Marie Vaublanc defends the return of the Ancien Régime order, and, implicitly, of slavery.
May:	L'Ouverture promoted by Sonthonax to commander in chief of French army in St-Domingue.
August:	Toussaint forces Sonthonax to leave St-Domingue and return to France.

1798

April:	Toussaint negotiates with General Thomas Maitland for British withdrawal from St-Domingue. Toussaint takes over Port-au-Prince.
October:	Toussaint expels French Commissioner Hédouville from the colony. Hédouville transfers his authority to the mixed-race general Rigaud, escalating a tense standoff with Toussaint. Toussaint successfully sends a trade mission to the United States, stoking suspicions that he seeks independence for the colony. St-Domingue is effectively under British and American naval protection from French warships.
November:	Toussaint orders all non-enlisted adult blacks to return to plantations for obligatory wage labour.

1799

July:	Toussaint and Rigaud enter into open conflict ('War of the Knives'). Toussaint narrowly escapes multiple assassination attempts by Rigaud's followers.
November:	Siege of Jacmel by Dessalines. French Directory collapses, Bonaparte takes dictatorial power as First Consul in France. New French constitution declares the colonies to be ruled by 'special laws', implying the return of slavery.

1800
August: Rigaud, defeated by L'Ouverture, flees to France.

October: L'Ouverture decrees military-enforced obligatory
               labour policy. L'Ouverture's adoptive nephew Moyse
               calls for smallholding land reform, supporting blacks
               in a revolt against forced plantation labour and
               returning white landowners, claiming the life of
               Bayon de Libertat. Toussaint arrests and executes
               Moyse.

1801
January: Toussaint invades and takes control of Spanish Santo
               Domingo. He rules the island of Hispaniola
               unopposed. St-Domingue begins to return to
               economic prosperity.

May: Toussaint unilaterally promulgates a constitution for
               St-Domingue, codifying the universal abolition of
               slavery and prohibiting all racial discrimination, while
               simultaneously naming himself dictatorial governor
               for life.

July–
October: Both the United States and Britain inform France
               that they are opposed to the independence of St-
               Domingue and will not interfere with an invasion to
               depose L'Ouverture.

1802
February: French fleet carrying 21,000 troops led by Emmanuel
               Leclerc arrives in St-Domingue. On Toussaint's
               order, Henry Christophe burns the capital city of
               Cap Français to the ground.

February–
March: Fighting inflicts heavy casualties on both sides.

April: Henry Christophe joins Leclerc's forces with some
               1,200 troops.

May: Toussaint offers to surrender to Leclerc. Napoleon
               promulgates the reintroduction of slavery in the
               French overseas colonies.

July: News arrives in St-Domingue of the reintroduction of slavery in Guadeloupe; a massive uprising follows against the French.

August: Toussaint is arrested by Leclerc in Gonaïves and deported to Fort de Joux, France.

September: General Caferelli interrogates Toussaint in his prison cell, hoping to gain information on riches Toussaint had putatively hidden in St-Domingue.

October: Leclerc dies of yellow fever, joining the 50,000 French troops lost since February – out of a total of some 80,000 – to fighting and disease in St-Domingue.

1803
January: Toussaint weakens and grows ill in his prison cell.

7 April: Toussaint L'Ouverture dies in prison in France from a respiratory infection, malnutrition, and exposure to the elements.

May: Britain declares war on France; the French position in St-Domingue becomes untenable.

June: British forces blocade St-Domingue.

31
December: Declaration of the independence of Haiti.

NOTE ON THE TEXTS

The correspondence of Toussaint L'Ouverture is vast, and remains to a great degree unpublished, dispersed across the globe in various archives and private collections, awaiting a critical edition (see David Geggus, *Haitian Revolutionary Studies*, Indiana University Press, 2002). The small selection of letters the editors of this volume have chosen seeks to present to the Anglophone reader a representative sample of L'Ouverture's writings.

These letters testify to the leadership of Toussaint L'Ouverture in the Haitian Revolution (1791–1804), as well as describing one of the most astounding instances of political subjectivation in human history. Toussaint L'Ouverture started life as a slave, and after 1776 became a free and slave-owning black. In a few short years after 1789, however, he reinvented himself to become the world-famous figure who transformed what had begun as one more colonial revolt into a world-historical sequence that initiated global decolonization and the destruction of plantation slavery. By 1801 he had led St-Domingue to de facto independence, simultaneously inventing the concept of associated statehood.[1]

The editors have chosen this selection of writings with an eye to conveying Toussaint's rhetorical, theoretical and military genius. They bear witness to the manner in which he focused the Haitian Revolution around a single, non-negotiable struggle: the universal, immediate and unqualified emancipation from slavery of all human beings. He did so at a time when there existed no available model for such political claims in the Atlantic world. In the United States, only a very few gradual emancipation laws had been promulgated by 1793; all were laws that subordinated the immediate interests of slaves to the defence of the rights of property owners. In revolutionary France, slavery would only be abolished under duress in February 1794, when general liberty had already been a de facto reality in St-Domingue for some three years, and a de jure one since the previous August.

Toussaint was fluent in both Kreyol and French, and, like his counterpart Napoleon, he dictated and rewrote all of his letters with a team of French and mulatto secretaries. Deborah Jenson has shown how, in this manner, he strove to 'spin' public perception of the revolution in St-Domingue.[2] One contemporary account reveals how this largely illiterate former slave actively transformed himself into a prominent figure and public intellectual of the French Revolution:

> I saw him in few words verbally lay out the summary of his addresses [to his secretaries]; rework the poorly conceived, poorly executed sentences; confront several secretaries presenting their work by turns; redo the ineffective sections; transpose parts to place them to better effect; making himself worthy, all in all, of the natural genius foretold by Raynal.[3]

Incredibly, Toussaint would dictate as many as 300 letters in a single day.[4]

When Toussaint L'Ouverture made his first public announcement, on 29 August 1793, that he would lead the struggle to make 'liberty and equality reign in St-Domingue', he autonomously drew his own conclusions from the 1789 *Déclaration des Droits de l'homme et du Citoyen*. All those benefiting from the slave-holding system, including not only whites in France and the colonies, but also mulattos and even free blacks, had unanimously avoided invoking the cause of human rights in their struggle for hegemony over the unfolding French Revolution. In France, only Mirabeau had had the clarity and courage to deduce from the universal claims of the Rights of Man that 'any man, whatever his color, has an equal right to liberty'.[5]

Like his French counterparts, Sièyes, Mirabeau, Danton and above all Robespierre, Toussaint's correspondence shows the development of a tactical mastery in the art of communication. He developed this mastery in the context of a transformation in the nature of political power in 1790s France, when mastery over symbolic political capital – the rhetoric of Liberty, Equality and Fraternity – itself became a means of winning political power.[6] Toussaint was able to assert hegemony over the unfolding events in St-Domingue because he combined the strategic military genius he has always been granted with a spontaneous and virtuosic grasp of the powerful role the ideology of universal human rights had suddenly come to play in international politics since 25 August 1789.

For Toussaint L'Ouverture and the former slaves of St-Domingue, the 'liberty' and 'equality' of 1789 were not *only* the ideological falsehoods of the bourgeoisie's bid for power that Marx would later assail. They also offered a previously inconceivable opportunity to upset the (symbolic) economy of the eighteenth-century world-system. In their very emptiness, these concepts harboured a latent operative efficacy. The signifier 'general liberty' thus opened a gap or interval in that century, a gap inherent in the inadequation between the slaves' political exclusion and the 'universal' rights of man. To witness the politicization of Toussaint L'Ouverture and the Haitian Revolution today is to initiate a genealogy of the process of political subjectivation – an inquiry essential to any conceivable progress towards emancipation.[7]

Nick Nesbitt
Centre for Modern Thought, University of Aberdeen
June 2008

I

PROCLAMATION

29 August 1793

Toussaint Bréda issued this, his first public proclamation, from Camp Turel. It announced both his adoption of the name L'Ouverture and his alignment with the cause of general liberty that would soon radicalize the French Revolution to include blacks within the compass of the Rights of Man and Citizen. His formulation of the relation between liberty and equality is radical and uncompromising: liberty and equality are inseparable, and to achieve them will require subordinating a plurality of competing demands within a unified struggle to destroy plantation slavery.

Brothers and Friends,

Remember the brave Ogé,[1] dear comrades, who was killed for having defended the cause of liberty! Yes, he died: but those who were his judges are now his defenders. I am Toussaint L'Ouverture; perhaps my name has made itself known to you. You know, brothers, that I have undertaken this vengeance, and that I want liberty and equality to reign in St-Domingue.[2] I have worked since the beginning [of the revolt] to make that happen, and to bring happiness to all. Unite yourselves to us, brothers, and fight with us for the same cause. [. . .] You say that you are fighting for liberty and equality? Is it possible that we could destroy ourselves, one against the other, and all fighting for the same cause? It is I who have undertaken [this struggle] and I wish to fight until it [liberty] exists [. . .] among us. Equality cannot exist without liberty. And for liberty to exist, we must have unity.

2

LETTER TO BIASSOU

15 October 1791

In autumn 1791, two months after the beginning of the uprising, Toussaint left his home at the Bréda plantation to join the forces led by Biassou. Toussaint already addressed Biassou as an equal at this stage, and from the tone of this letter seems already to have achieved a level of authority at least equal to that of the other leaders, Dutty Boukman and Jean-François. The letter refers to a planned attack on Cap Français that never took place.

Grande Riviere
15 October 1791

To M. Biassou, brigadier of the King's Army at Grand Boucan

My very dear friend
In keeping with the request I just made of the Spanish and daily awaiting the thing I asked for, I beg of you to wait until we are in a better state before going on to what you have the kindness to write me about. I have too much of a wish to go, but in all the habitations I would like to have crowbars in order to have the rocks of the mountains of Haut du Cap fall to prevent them [the slave-owners' forces] from approaching us for I think they have

no other means without exposing their people to a slaughter. I ask that you make sure with the spy you have sent to have him clearly explain where the powder works are in Haut du Cap so we can succeed in taking the powder works. Thus, my friend, you can see whether I took precautions in this affair, and you can tell this to Bouqueman [Boukman]. As for Jean François he can still go in a carriage with his ladies, but he hasn't done me the honour of writing to me for several days. I am very surprised by this. If you need tafia [rum-like liquor] I will send you some when you'd like, but try to use it sparingly. The troops must not be given this so they won't get out of hand. Send me a few barrows for I need them to transport wood to put up the cabins at the tannery for my people.

I ask you to assure your mother and sister of my humble respect.

I have the honour, my dear friend, of being your very humble, obedient servant.

General Doctor

3

LETTER TO THE GENERAL ASSEMBLY FROM BIASSOU, JEAN-FRANÇOIS AND TOUSSAINT L'OUVERTURE

July 1792

This extraordinary document, signed by Toussaint in the name of his fourteen-year-old nephew Belair, was written by the leaders of the slave revolt to the colonial assembly in St-Domingue and the national commissioner Roume. After failed negotiations six months before, the letter testifies to an early and rapid radicalization of the revolution to encompass the call for general liberty based on the logic of indivisible, universal human rights.

Gentlemen,

Those who have the honour to present you with these memoirs are a class of men whom up to the present you have failed to recognize as like yourselves, and whom you have covered in opprobrium by heaping upon them the ignominy attached to their unfortunate lot. These are men who don't know how to choose big words, but who are going to show you and all the world the justice of their cause; finally, they are those whom you call your slaves and who claim the rights to which all men may aspire.

For too long, gentlemen, by way of abuses that one can never too strongly accuse of having taken place because of our lack of understanding and our ignorance – for a very long time, I say – we have been victims of your greed and your avarice. Under the blows of your barbarous whip we have accumulated for you the treasures you enjoy in this colony; the human race has suffered to see with what barbarity you have treated men like yourself – yes, men – over whom you have no other right except that you are stronger and more barbaric than we; you have engaged in [slave] traffic, you have sold men for horses, and even that is the least of your shortcomings in the eyes of humanity; our lives depend on your caprice, and when it's a question of amusing yourselves, the burden falls on men like us, who most often are guilty of no other crime than to be under your orders.

We are black, it is true, but tell us, gentlemen, you who are so judicious, what is the law that says that the black man must belong to and be the property of the white man? Certainly you will not be able to make us see where that exists, if it is not in your imaginations – always ready to form new [phantasms] so long as they are to your advantage. Yes, gentlemen, we are free like you, and it is only by your avarice and our ignorance that anyone is still held in slavery up to this day, and we can neither see nor find the right that you pretend to have over us, nor anything that could prove it to us, set down on the earth like you, all being children of the same father created in the same image. We are your equals then, by natural right, and if nature pleases itself to diversify colours within the human race, it is not a crime to be born black nor an advantage to be white. If the abuses in the Colony have gone on for several years, that was before the fortunate revolution that has taken place in the motherland, which has opened for us the road which our courage and labour will enable us to ascend, to arrive at the temple of liberty, like those brave Frenchmen who are our models and whom all the universe is contemplating.

For too long we have borne your chains without thinking of shaking them off, but any authority which is not founded on virtue and humanity, and which only tends to subject one's fellow man to slavery, must come to an end, and that end is yours. You, gentlemen, who pretend to subject us to slavery – have you not sworn to uphold the French Constitution? What does it say, this respectable constitution? What is the fundamental law? Have you forgotten that you have formally vowed the Declaration of the Rights of Man, which says that men are born free, equal in their rights; that their natural rights include liberty, property, security and resistance to oppression? So then, as you cannot deny what you have sworn, we are within our rights, and you ought to recognize yourselves as perjurers; by your decrees you recognize that all men are free, but you want to maintain servitude for 480,000 individuals who allow you to enjoy all that you possess. Through your envoys you offer liberty only to our chiefs; it is still one of your maxims of politics to say that those who have played an equal part in our work should be delivered by us to be your victims. No, we prefer a thousand deaths to acting that way towards our own kind. If you want to accord us the benefits that are due to us, they must also shower onto all of our brothers . . .

Gentlemen, in very few words you have seen our way of thinking – it is unanimous and it is after consulting everyone to whom we are connected in the same cause that we present to you our demands, as follows.

First: general liberty for all men detained in slavery.

Second: general amnesty for the past.

Third: the guarantee of these articles by the Spanish government.

Fourth: the three articles above are the basis and the sole means to achieve a peace that would be respected by the two parties, and only after they are approved in the name of the Colony and M. the Lieutenant Général, and when the National Civil Commissioners have agreed to present this approval to the king, and to the National Assembly.

If, like us, you desire that the articles above be accepted, we will commit ourselves to the following: first, to lay down our arms; second, that each of us will return to the plantation to which he belongs and resume his work on condition of a wage which will be set by the year for each cultivator who starts work for a fixed term.

Here, gentlemen, is the request of men who are like you, and here is their final resolution: they are resolved to live free or die.

We have the honour to be, gentlemen, your very humble and obedient servants.

Biassou, Jean-François, Belair

4

LETTER TO GENERAL LAVEAUX

18 May 1794

Toussaint refused to rally to the French republican cause until the French abolished slavery in February 1794. In this his first letter to the French general, Toussaint accounts for his previous decision to fight on with the Spanish forces until May.

Marmelade, 18 May 1794

Toussaint L'Ouverture, General of the Western Army, to Etienne Laveaux, interim Governor General

[. . .] It is true, General, that I have been led into error by the enemies of the Republic and humanity, but what man can flatter himself to have avoided all the traps of evil men? In truth, I fell into their nets, not without knowing what I was doing; you will remember that [. . .] my goal was only that we unite to combat the enemies of France and to bring an end to an internal war among the French of this colony. Unfortunately for all concerned, the paths toward reconciliation that I suggested were rejected. My heart bled and I shed tears over the unfortunate fate of my country, foreseeing the misfortunes that would follow, and in this I was not mistaken. Fatal experience has shown the truth of my predictions.[1]

At the time, the Spanish offered me their protection and freedom for all those who fought for the cause of kings. Having always fought to achieve this same liberty, I accepted their offer, seeing myself abandoned by the French, my brothers. But a somewhat late experience opened my eyes to these perfidious protectors. Having perceived their treachery, I saw clearly that they intended for us to set upon each other to diminish our number and to enchain those who remained to return them to their former slavery. No, never would they achieve their infamous goal! And we will have revenge on these contemptible beings in our turn in every way. Let us unite forever, therefore, and, forgetting the past, let us seek henceforth only to crush our enemies and to avenge ourselves against our treacherous neighbours.

It is true that the national flag flies over Gonaïves and its surroundings, and that I have routed the Spanish and emigrants from the area. But my heart is broken to contemplate the event that occurred against a few unfortunate whites who were victims in this affair. I am utterly unlike many others who witness scenes of horror in cold blood. I have always held humanity in common to all, and I suffer whenever I cannot prevent evil. There were also a number of uprisings in the workshops, but I rapidly returned things to order and all are working as before.

Gonaïves, Gros-Morne, the canton of Ennery, Marmelade, Plaisance, Dondon, Acul, and all of Limbé are under my orders, and I count four thousand armed men in these areas, without counting the citizens of Gros-Morne, who number six hundred. As to war munitions, I am entirely bereft, having consumed them in the various attacks that I made against the enemy. [. . .]

Salvation in the fatherland,

Toussaint L'Ouverture

5

LETTER TO LAVEAUX

7 July 1794

By the summer of 1794, Spanish and British forces still occupied territory in the east, but the republican forces had defeated the Spanish in the west of St-Domingue. In July, Toussaint L'Ouverture defeated the rebel leader Jean-François, who was still siding with the Spanish.

Marmelade

Toussaint L'Ouverture, General of the Western Army, to Etienne Laveaux, interim Governor General of the French section of St-Domingue

I write to share with you the success I have had in the last three to four days against general Jean-François in Dondon. He had been sent to Fort Dauphin to combat me. In fact, he did attack my troops on various occasions during my stay in Port Magot, but he was always repulsed vigorously. Finally, upon my return, I felt in a position to attack him. Having taken my bearings, I attacked simultaneously Dondon, the Fort, and other posts. These were taken with sabre in hand. I very nearly captured Jean-François; he owed his salvation to the thickness of the bushes he threw himself into in desperation, leaving his clothes behind him. I captured all his affairs and papers. He saved only his shirt and pants. My troops made a carnage of his men and I took many prisoners. [. . .]

I also read of the September sessions of this last year of the National Convention and the decree they issued for the abolition of slavery. This is reassuring news for friends of humanity, and I hope that in the future all will feel more at ease and that, if we are able to enjoy peace and tranquility, the colony will flourish to an unparalleled degree. [. . .]

I hope that we may meet to discuss our affairs together. Let me know the day and place that I may be there. [. . .]

Salvation in the fatherland, and its success,

Toussaint L'Ouverture

6

TOUSSAINT L'OUVERTURE TO HIS BROTHERS AND SISTERS IN VARETTES

22 March 1795

Brothers and Sisters

The moment has arrived when the veil obscuring the light must fall. You should never again forget the decrees of the National Convention. Its principles, its love for freedom, are invariable, and henceforth there can exist no possibility of the destruction of this sacred edifice.

I learned with infinite joy of the return of the citizens of Upper Varettes within the Republic. There they will find the happiness they had fled at the instigation of the soldiers of tyranny and royalty.

To give them support, to console them of their past faults and to lead them to abjure the errors they nourished insidiously, is for all republicans an absolute duty and the sacred maxim of the French.

It is for this reason not only because of the powers confided in me by General Laveaux, but even more so because I am animated by feelings of humanity and fraternity, that I remind the citizens of Upper Varettes of their mistakes. But as much as they may harm the interests of the Republic, I do sense that their return, if it is sincere, can be an advantage helping towards our success.

The French are our brothers, the English, the Spanish, and the royalists are ferocious beasts who only caress to suck at their leisure, until they are satiated, the blood of their women and children.

Citizens, I do not wish here to describe your wrong actions further; I have at all times considered them as no more than errors. You have returned to the Republic, and so the past is now forgotten. Your duty is now to contribute with all your moral and physical might to strengthen your parish and to make flourish therein the principles of holy liberty. If it is otherwise, do not hope for any further signs of our fraternity. Think well about what I am saying.

It is in these circumstances that I have ordered and order the following:

First Article – All citizens united under the flag of the French nation, whether in the parish of Varettes or in the Republican camps of the Western Line, are and will remain under the safety and protection of the law. It is forbidden to slander or do harm to them.

Second Article – The conservation of citizens' properties is assured by the constitution; consequently, all the commanders of the parishes, camps and posts of the line are ordered to respect and preserve these, and this, under their personal responsibility.

[. . .]

Fifth Article – All farmers, twenty-four hours after the publication of the present proclamation, shall return to pursue all forms of agricultural labour in the plantations to which they are dependent, except those contiguous with enemy territory. The cultivators of plantations bordering the enemy, if they are not soldiers, will report to other plantations to participate in labour.

Sixth Article – Work is necessary, it is a virtue. It is the general good of the state. Every lazy and errant man will be arrested to be punished by the law. But service is also conditional and will be paid a just wage.

7

LETTER TO JEAN-FRANÇOIS

13 June 1795

While Toussaint joined the French Republican forces in the summer of 1794, Jean-François continued to fight for the Spanish. In his attempt to rally the citizens of Dondon to the Spanish, Jean-François told them that 'there is no irrevocable liberty for the former slaves except that which the Spanish monarch would grant them because, as a legitimate king, he alone has the right to legitimate that freedom'.[1] This letter is Toussaint's response to that claim.

1. It would seem from the first article of your pronouncement that republicans have offered to give themselves up to you. Should there exist among us men cowardly enough to take back their chains, we wilfully abandon them to you; they do not deserve to be our brothers.

2. You claim in your second article to show that we have been misled, while we hope to convince you that anyone who is a subject or vassal of kings is no more than a vile slave, and that a republican alone is truly a man.

3. Consequently we are free by natural right. It could only be kings, whose name alone expresses what is most vile and despicable, who could dare claim the right to reduce into servitude men made like them and whom nature has made free.

4. Should the republican party destroy all its enemies, as we have no doubt it will, it will have no need to adopt us anew; together we support a single, identical cause. [. . .]

5. You finish, vile slaves that you are, by offering us the protection of the king, your master. Discover and tell to Casa-Calvo [the Governor of Spanish Santo-Domingo] that republicans cannot come to agreement with a king. Let him come, and you with him; we are ready to receive you in the manner of republicans.

8

LETTER TO DIEUDONNÉ

12 February 1796

Dieudonné was an African-born leader who controlled some 3,000 soldiers in the mountains above Port-au-Prince. Born in the kingdom of the Kongo, he and his followers were by 1796 increasingly reluctant to submit to the mulatto leadership of Rigaud and Bauvais. Resenting the discrimination he felt he received from the latter, Dieudonné had begun negotiations with the British in late 1795. The following letter is Toussaint's attempt to prevent Dieudonné and his troops from defecting to the British.

Verettes, 23 Pluviôse, year IV of the French Republic, one and indivisible

Toussaint to Pierre Dieudonné

My dear brother and friend
I know that our friends the civil commissioners Polvérel and Sonthonax had the greatest confidence in you because you were a true republican. And so it is impossible for me to believe the slanderous rumours that have been spread about you: that you have abandoned your fatherland to join the English, the sworn enemies of our freedom and equality.

Is it possible, my dear friend, that in the moment when France has triumphed over all the royalists and, through its beneficent decree of 9 Thermidor, grants us all the rights for which we have been fighting, that you would let yourself be deceived by our former tyrants, who only exploit a group of our unfortunate brothers the better to enchain the others? Though the Spanish, for a certain time, attracted me, I quickly recognized their malevolence. I abandoned them and have since thoroughly defeated them. I returned to my fatherland which received me with open arms and has rewarded me for my services. I invite you, my dear brother, to follow my example. If for some reason you are unable to put your trust in generals Rigaud and Bauvais, Governor Laveaux, who is the father of us all and in whom the motherland has placed her trust, must also merit yours. I think as well that you will not refuse it to me, a black like yourself, and I assure you that I wish nothing else in the world than to see you happy, you and all our brothers. For my part, I believe that this is only possible by serving the French Republic; it is under its flag that we are truly free and equal. This is how I see things, my dear friend, and I don't believe I am mistaken.

If it had been possible for me to see you, I would have had the pleasure of embracing you, and I flatter myself that you wouldn't have refused me your friendship. You can trust what my three officers will tell you; it will be the truth. If, when they come, you wish to send me two or three of your own, we will speak together, and I am certain that what I will say to them will open their eyes. If it is possible that the English have managed to fool you, believe me, my dear brother, abandon them, unite with the good republicans, and, all together, let us rid our land of the royalists. They are scoundrels who wish to return us to the shameful chains that we had so much difficulty breaking. Despite everything that has been said about you, I have no doubt that you are a good republican; as such, you must unite with generals Rigaud and Bauvais who are good republicans, since our country has rewarded them for their services. Should you nonetheless have small disagreements, you should not fight against them, because the Republic, which is the mother of us all, does not wish us to fight our brothers. Moreover, it is always the poor people who suffer the most. When we leaders have disputes amongst ourselves, we should not have the soldiers in our charge fight one another. Instead, we should turn to our superiors who are there to render justice and bring us to agreement. Remember, my dear friend, that the French Republic is one and indivisible, that that is what constitutes its strength, and that it will vanquish all its enemies.

Believe me, my dear friend, forget all individual animosity, reunite with our brothers Rigaud and Bauvais. They are brave defenders of general liberty who love their fatherland too much not to desire with all their heart to be friends of you and all whom you command. [. . .]

I embrace you and salute you in the name of the fatherland, you and all our good brothers.

Toussaint L'Ouverture

9

LETTER TO LAVEAUX

20 February 1796

In February 1796, plantation workers in the northern mountains near Port-de-Paix revolted in response to the dismissal of Etienne Datty, a local black commander. Toussaint, who rode overnight to put down the rebellion, describes in this letter his negotiations with the rebels. The letter is particularly important in its examination of the diverse claims and definitions of freedom being made by the various communities united under the French flag. For Toussaint, freedom is only possible through organized labour under the rule of universal, rights-based law offered by the French Republic (in implicit contrast to the slave-holding Spanish and English states in competition for control of the island). For the rebellious workers, freedom arises instead through a shared communal experience of suffering such as that they have shared with Datty which has no necessary connection, and is even inimical, to large-scale plantation labour.

1 Ventôse, An 4

Toussaint L'Ouverture to Etienne Laveaux
[. . .] As soon as I arrived [in Port-de-Paix], I wrote to Pageot, commander of the Northern Province, to alert him to my arrival, and sent Baptiste Andro with two of my dragoons to deliver the letter. At that moment, a large number of farmers, both men and

women, came to me with food, some chickens and eggs. They told me how glad they were to see me and that they hoped I would put an end to all these disorders. I ordered them to get me hay, which they did immediately and seemed to do with pleasure. I took this to be a good sign that it would not be difficult to resolve things.

At seven in the evening, Etienne arrived, in conformity with the order I had sent him, with around five hundred men, many of them armed. I saddled my horse and ordered Etienne to form a circle of all the citizens who had gone with him, as well as those who had just arrived with the hay. I mounted my horse and entered the circle where, after having condemned the murders they had committed, I told them that if they wished to preserve their liberty they would have to submit to the laws of the Republic, and be docile and work, that it was only in this way that they would benefit from their freedom. Furthermore, I said that if they had any claim to make that they would never obtain it in this manner, and that God had said: Ask and ye shall receive, knock and my door will be open to you, but that he has not said to commit crimes to obtain what one needs.

I asked them if they knew me and whether they were glad to see me. They answered yes, that they knew that I was the father of all the blacks, and that they also knew that I had never ceased to work for their happiness and for their liberty, but they begged me to listen to them and that perhaps I would see that they perhaps were not so in the wrong as I believed. I was quiet and listened to them. One of them spoke and said to me: 'General, all of us look upon you as our father, it is you after God who are dearest to us and in whom we have the most confidence.' I told him to be silent and said that if they thought of me in this way they should not have acted as they had, and that if they had feared to address the Governor General [Laveaux] whom we must all regard as our father and the defender of our liberty, they should have come to me. I would then have tried to convince the Governor General to meet their demands if I found them just, and that I would in this way have prevented them from committing such crimes. They answered me that they love the Governor General, but that unfortunately for them, all men are not like him, for then they would surely be happy. They went on to say, 'Since the beginning of the revolution, Etienne has always been our leader, it is he who has always commanded us. He has always shared in our misery in our struggle to win our freedom. Why has his command been taken from him, and why is he seen as so undeserving as to give it to another without our agreement? That is why, general, we took up arms. It is unfortunate for us that there are bad men among us who have committed crimes. But we are by no means accomplices in all that. Alas, general, they wish as well to make us slaves; there is no equality here, as it seems there is with you. Look how the whites and coloured men who are with you are good and are united with the blacks. One would think they were brothers from the same mother. That, general, is what we call equality. Here it is not the same. We are looked down upon, they vex us at every turn. They don't pay us what we are owed for the food we grow. They force us to give away our chickens and pigs for nothing when we go to sell them in the city, and if we complain, they have us arrested by the police, and they throw us in prison without giving us anything to eat, and then make us pay to get out. You see, general, that one is not free if he is treated like this. We are certain from what we observe that all those who are with you are content and love you.'

When he stopped speaking, I asked him if this was all they had to complain about. He answered me: 'Yes.' I asked all the others if what he had said was true. They answered me all together that it was true. I quieted them down and said, 'My friends, I shouldn't treat you in this way, because the shame you bring to me and all the men of our colour makes me see that you are not my friends. All the reasons that you give appear just to me, but if you should give me a house full of them' – I used this expression to make them understand that they could have all the reasons they wished and still they were in the wrong because they had rendered themselves guilty in the eyes of God, of the law, and of men. 'What will I tell the National Convention when it will ask me for an account of what you have just done? How is it possible, when I have just sent deputies to the National Convention to thank them in the name of all the blacks for the magnanimous decree that grants them liberty? How can I assure them, after this, that they will work to deserve this decree and will prove to France and to all nations that they are worthy by their submission to the law, by their work and their docility, that I can answer for them all, and that soon, with the help of France, we shall prove to the entire universe that St-Domingue, worked by free hands, will recover its wealth? Answer me this. My shame will show that I have deceived them; it will prove to them what the enemies of our freedom have tried to make them believe, that blacks are not fit to be free, that if they become free they will no longer work, and that they will steal and kill.'

They answered me that they were wrong and begged me, in all my friendship for them, to repair this mistake, and swore to me never to do wrong again and to be wise and obedient, to do nothing more without consulting me and to stop the first among them who would dare to give bad advice. They said to me as well that it was absolutely essential that I put things back in order before leaving, that I had come too far not to leave them in peace before returning. I promised them that I had come for nothing else, but that it was up to them to prove that they wanted peace and tranquillity by all of them returning immediately to their respective plantations and starting back to work, and that this was entirely up to them. They answered me in a single voice: 'Forgive us, general, we will be so good that you will be forced to forget what we have just done.' So I asked them to go away. To Etienne I said that these were not all the citizens of his parish.

He answered me that no, there were still three camps in the mountains. After that, I said to all those I had just sent away to return the next day when those from the mountains had arrived, that I wished to pardon them all together.

It was 9.30 in the evening. I asked Etienne where his secretary was. He said to me that he was also in the mountains. I ordered Etienne to give him the order to return to the plantation with all the citizens who were camped in the mountains to see me.

[. . .]

LETTER TO FLAVILLE

This letter is Toussaint's attempt to defuse growing tensions between himself and the mulattos in northern St-Domingue. In January 1795, some 180 of Toussaint's troops had defected to his rival Villatte, who controlled the area around Cap Français. In June, Joseph Flaville and his troops joined Villatte. On 20 March 1796, these troops entered into open rebellion against Toussaint when they took Laveaux prisoner. After rescuing the latter, Toussaint strove to reinforce unity among the various factions fighting the English and Spanish (African-born Bossales, blacks like himself born in St-Domingue, and mixed-race mulattos). The letter is in response to an apology from Flaville, who had written in defeat to Toussaint: 'Let us live united in brotherhood, so that nothing can trouble the harmony that must exist among good republicans.'

Toussaint L'Ouverture, Commander of the Western Line, to Joseph Flaville, Commander of Acul

I received your letter of 8 Messidor; previously, I had received that of my colleague Villatte. From that moment on I felt no more hatred. I know that you were under the command of our brother, and am glad of it. Your wrong was great: you were under orders at the Cap and you reported to me in everything.

That being the case, my dear Flaville, you should have made me aware of your commission so that I would have left you alone under the command of my colleague Villatte.

You know me, my dear Joseph Flaville, you know the flexibility of my heart, always ready to pardon. I wish to believe in your sincerity, but, to reassure myself, I only ask (and it is right to do so) that all the troops whom you have led astray and who have taken up arms against me return to their posts as before. This in order that the disobedience into which you have plunged them be transformed into a perfect submission, and that you make them aware that it was through your own fault that they fell into disobedience, and that you now understand that the lack of discipline in the troops is the mother of all its vices and that an undisciplined troop is lost. [. . .]

I wish to live in peace, united with my brothers.

Greetings and friendship

Toussaint L'Ouverture

II

ADDRESS TO SOLDIERS FOR THE UNIVERSAL DESTRUCTION OF SLAVERY

18 May 1797

Let the sacred flame of liberty that we have won lead all our acts. [. . .] Let us go forth to plant the tree of liberty, breaking the chains of those of our brothers still held captive under the shameful yoke of slavery. Let us bring them under the compass of our rights, the imprescriptible and inalienable rights of free men. [Let us overcome] the barriers that separate nations, and unite the human species into a single brotherhood. We seek only to bring to men the liberty that [God] has given them, and that other men have taken from them only by transgressing His immutable will.

Bulletin officiel de St-Domingue, 18 May 1797

12

LETTER TO LAVEAUX

23 May 1797

This letter is addressed to Laveaux as the representative of St-Domingue in the French Assembly, where Toussaint had dispatched him to defend the interests of the colony and through him the legislature against the forces of reaction, as well as (presumably) to give himself a freer hand to rule over the colony. L'Ouverture goes to considerable lengths in this letter to convince Laveaux, and the Legislature, of his fidelity to France and, by implication, his lack of interest in declaring the colony independent

Gonaïves, 4 prairial, year 5 of the French Republic, one and indivisible

Toussaint L'Ouverture to Etienne Laveaux, Representative of the People, Deputy of St-Domingue in the Legislature

My dear Representative

Since your departure and to this day, I am still denied the sweet satisfaction of receiving your news. I have written to you a number of times, and remain uncertain whether my letters have reached you unhindered. May this one reach you as promptly as I desire. [. . .]

The perfect harmony, tranquillity and union that reign among us portend happy success in our future endeavours, and I can only believe that with the help of God we shall soon purge the French territory of the tyrannical hordes who have infested the colony for too long, and that soon we will form a single, unified family of friends and brothers.

It would be in vain for the enemies of France still to seek to undermine the cause that the republicans who live here defend. The colony's survival is guaranteed. Please convey to the Legislature the nature of my efforts and my sincere attachment, describing to them how such an important portion of France as this colony must no longer be deprived of the aid she owes it, and that the enemies of France and general liberty have kept from it by distorting the true position of St-Domingue. Its preservation, let me repeat, is assured, and [France] can count upon my irrevocable zeal as its true defender.

I have just been promoted by the Commission of the French government to the rank of General in Chief of St-Domingue. Inspired by a love of the public good and the happiness of my citizens, I am not blinded by such honours, and remain steadfast in the important task that has been confided in me. My time and attention will be fully occupied in seeking to merit the support of the Legislature and of my fellow citizens. My wishes will be granted and my compensation ideal if, with the help of God, I am happy enough to be able, after having expelled the enemies of the colony, soon to say to France: the flag of liberty flies across the surface of St-Domingue. [. . .]

How sweet it would be for me, my dear Representative, to be able to correspond with you as frequently as I desire it and to receive from you more often your dear news, if the communication between France and the colonies were not so hindered. Seize every occasion, I beg of you, to give me this satisfaction, which will always be, as you know, infinitely sweet to me.

I send into your care my beloved children, whom I miss dearly. May God look over their days and bestow upon them His grace, that they may profit from the education that France grants them, to render themselves one day worthy of expressing their gratitude! Kiss them tenderly for me and on behalf of their mother, and do send me news of them at the nearest occasion.

May you remain, I repeat to you and beseech you, in the name of the salvation of the colony, in the name of its prosperity and tranquillity that reappear here daily, the true defender of its rights, by striking down its enemies who, through vain stratagems, continue to seek to distract the favourable gaze of France from her colony, which today more than ever must remain fixated upon it. Reassure her of the preservation of this colony, by all that we hold dear, and by all that she may expect of our courage and devotion. She may be certain that so long as the blood flows in our veins, we shall only strive for the defence of the colony and of liberty, and to cast away all agitators and enemies.

In reiterating to you in particular the devotion that you have inspired in me, I ask you to transmit my feelings of respect and those of my wife to your own wife and dear family, and be certain that the ties of our friendship will only terminate with the end of my days.

Greetings and friendship

Toussaint L'Ouverture

13

LETTER TO THE FRENCH DIRECTORY

November 1797

This letter, along with his 1793 proclamation the most famous Toussaint ever wrote, is the culminating document of his republican political philosophy and his steadfast defence of universal human rights. It was written in response to the increasing conservatism of the French Directory, and, in particular, the attacks against Toussaint by the arch-racist, pro-slavery representative Vaublanc.[1]

Toussaint L'Ouverture to the French Directory

When the people of St-Domingue first tasted the fruit of liberty that they hold from the equity of France; when to the violent upheavals of the revolution that announced it succeeded the pleasures of tranquillity; when finally the rule of law took the place of anarchy under which the unfortunate colony had too long suffered, what fatality can have led the greatest enemy of its prosperity and of our happiness still to dare to threaten us with the return of slavery? The impolitic and incendiary speech of Vaublanc has threatened the blacks less than the certainty of the plans meditated upon by the property owners of St-Domingue.

Such insidious declamations should have no effect upon the wise legislators who have decreed liberty to humanity. The attacks the colonists propose against this liberty must be feared all the more insofar as they hide their detestable projects under the veil of patriotism. We know that illusory and specious descriptions have been made to you of the renewal of terrible violence. Already, perfidious emissaries have crept among us to foment destruction at the hands of liberticides. They will not succeed, this I swear by all that is most sacred in liberty. My attachment to France, the gratitude that all the blacks conserve for her, make it my duty to hide from you neither the plans being fomented nor the oath that we renew to bury ourselves beneath the ruins of a country revived by liberty rather than suffer the return of slavery.

It is for you, Citizen Directors, to remove from over our heads the storm that the eternal enemies of our liberty are preparing in the shades of silence. It is for you to enlighten the Legislature, it is for you to prevent the enemies of the present system from spreading themselves on our unfortunate shores to sully them with new crimes. Do not allow our brothers, our friends, to be sacrificed to men who wish to reign over the ruins of the human species. But no, your wisdom will enable you to avoid the dangerous snares which our common enemies hold out for you. [. . .]

I send you with this letter a declaration which will acquaint you with the unity that exists between the proprietors of St-Domingue who are in France, those in the United States, and those who serve under the English banner. You will see there a resolution, unequivocal and carefully constructed, for the restoration of slavery; you will see there that their determination to succeed has led them to envelop themselves in the mantle of liberty in order to strike it more deadly blows. You will see that they are counting heavily on my willingness to espouse perfidious views out of fear for my children. It is not astonishing that these men who sacrifice their country to their interests are unable to conceive how many sacrifices a true love of country can support in a better father than they, since I unhesitatingly base the happiness of my children on that of my country, which they and they alone wish to destroy.

I shall never hesitate in choosing between the safety of St-Domingue and my personal happiness, but I have nothing to fear. It is to the solicitude of the French government that I have confided my children. [. . .] I would tremble with horror if it was into the hands of the colonists that I had sent them as hostages; but even if it were so, let them know that in punishing them for the fidelity of their father, they would only add one degree more to their barbarism, without any hope of making me fail in my duty. [. . .]

Blind as they are, they cannot see how this odious conduct on their part can become the signal of new disasters and irreparable misfortunes, and that far from it helping them regain what in their eyes liberty for all has made them lose, they expose themselves to total ruin and the colony to its inevitable destruction. Could men who have once enjoyed the benefits of liberty look on calmly while it is taken from them! They bore their chains when they knew no condition of life better than that of slavery. But today when they have left it, if they had a thousand lives, they would sacrifice them all rather than to be subjected again to slavery. But no, the hand that has broken our chains will not subject us to them again. France will not renounce her principles. She shall not permit the perversion of her sublime morality and the destruction of the principles that honour her the most, and the degradation of her most beautiful accomplishment, by rescinding the decree of 16 Pluviôse [4 February 1794, abolishing slavery in the French colonies] that honours so well all of humanity. But if, in order to re-establish servitude in St-Domingue this were to be done, I declare to you that this would be to attempt the impossible. We have known how to confront danger to obtain our liberty, and we will know how to confront death to preserve it. This, Citizens and Directors, is the morality of the people of St-Domingue, these are the principles I transmit to you on their behalf.

Let me renew to you the oath that I have made: to cease to exist before gratitude is stricken from my heart and to remain faithful to France, to my duty, and before the land of liberty be profaned and blackened by the liberticides, before they can wrest from my hands this glaive, these arms that France has confided in me for the defence of her rights, for those of humanity, and for the triumph of liberty and equality.

Greetings and respect

Toussaint L'Ouverture

14

BONAPARTE'S LETTER TO ST-DOMINGUE

25 December 1799

This letter in support of Napoleon's new constitution sought to placate blacks suspicious that it constituted a first step towards the reinstatement of slavery. Its promulgation of particular, differential legal status for the colonies, in distinction to the universalism of Republican law and the Declaration of the Rights of Man and of the Citizen, hearkened back to Ancien Régime differentialism. 'Special laws' had historically meant those laws allowing for slavery in the colonies. Reassurances of the 'SACRED' principles of freedom and equality had long rang hollow for Toussaint and his colleagues; indeed, his refusal to join the French after Sonthonax's unilateral declaration of abolition in 1793, and his decision to wait until the gesture was codified in national law are indicative of such a politics of suspicion. The paternalistic, almost obsequious tone of the text must have further encouraged such suspicion. This proved to be well-founded; Napoleon reinstated slavery in the French colonies in May 1802, and when news of this act reached St-Domingue, it radicalized the movement for universal emancipation to lead directly to the final defeat of the French and the independence of Haiti in 1804.

Paris, 4 Nivôse, year VIII

Citizens, a constitution that wasn't able to sustain itself against multiple violations has been replaced by a new pact destined to solidify freedom.

Article 91 states that French colonies will be ruled by special laws.

This disposition derives from the nature of things and the differences in climate.

The inhabitants of French colonies located in America, Asia and Africa cannot be governed by the same laws.

The differences in habits, in mores, in interests; the diversity of soil, crops and goods produced demand diverse modifications.

Far from being a subject of alarm for you, you will recognize here the wisdom and profundity of vision that animate the legislators of France.

The Consuls of the Republic, in announcing to you the new social pact, declare to you that the SACRED principles of the freedom and equality of blacks will NEVER SUFFER among you the least attack or modification.

If there are ill-intentioned men in the colony, if there are those who still have relations with enemy powers, remember BRAVE BLACKS, that the French people alone recognize your freedom and the equality of your rights.

The First Consul, BONAPARTE

15

PROCLAMATION ON LABOUR

1800

The tortuous logic and grammar of this proclamation are perhaps indicative of the contradictions of Toussaint's position. His various attempts to force the former slave population he putatively represented to engage in plantation labour they reasonably equated with their prior enslavement progressively led him to a position of paternalistic authoritarianism.

You will realize, citizens, that agriculture supports governments, because it promotes commerce, comfort and abundance, gives birth to the arts and industry, and keeps all occupied. It is the mechanism of all states, and if each member of society works, the result is public tranquillity; troubles disappear along with idleness, which is the mother of vice, and each enjoys in peace the fruits of his labours. [. . .] It is a fact that to ensure freedom, without which man cannot be happy, it is necessary for all to occupy themselves usefully in order to contribute to the public good and general tranquillity . . . Since the revolution, farmers, both men and women, who, since they were young at the time, were not engaged in farming, do not wish today to take part in it because, they say, they are free, and so spend their days running about aimlessly, thus setting a very bad example for the other farmers, while all the while generals, officers, their subordinates and soldiers are engaged in permanent activity to protect the sacred rights of all. [. . .][1]

16

SELF-PORTRAIT

1801

This short autobiographical statement passes over the fact that when the Revolution began in 1791, Toussaint had been a free man and even a slave-owner since at least 1776, and had accumulated a comfortable, though not extraordinary, amount of wealth in his name (see Geggus 2007). He had been taught to read and write at a basic level by Jesuits in the colony prior to 1789.

I felt that I was destined for great things. When I received this divine portent, I was fifty-four years old; I did not know how to read or write; I had a few *portugaises*; I gave them to a junior officer of the Regiment du Cap; and, thanks to him, in a few months I knew how to sign my name and read correctly.

The revolution of St-Domingue was going its way; I saw that the whites could not hold out, because they were divided among themselves and crushed by superior numbers; I congratulated myself on being black.

It was necessary to begin my career. I crossed into the Spanish region, where they had given asylum and protection to the first troops of my colour. This asylum and protection ended up nowhere; I was delighted to see Jean-François turn himself into a Spaniard at the moment when the powerful French Republic proclaimed the general freedom of the blacks. A secret voice said to me: 'Since the blacks are free, they need a chief', and it is I who must be the chief predicted by the Abbé Raynal. I returned, transported by this sentiment, to the service of France; France and the voice of God have not deceived me.

17

LETTER TO NAPOLEON ON THE 1801 CONSTITUTION

16 July 1801

27 Messidor, year IX

Citizen Consul

The Minister of the Navy, in the account he gave you of the political situation of this colony, which I devoted myself to making known to him, should have submitted to you my proclamation of last 16 Pluviôse [5 February 1801] on the convocation of a Central Assembly, which would be able to set the destiny of St-Domingue through wise laws modelled on the mores of its inhabitants. I today have the satisfaction of announcing to you that the final touch has just been put to this work. I hasten to send it to you in order to have your approval and the sanction of my government.

Given the absence of laws, and the Central Assembly having requested to have this constitution provisionally executed, which will more quickly lead St-Domingue to its future prosperity, I have surrendered to its wishes. This constitution was received by all classes of citizens with transports of joy that will not fail to be reproduced when it is sent back bearing the sanction of the government.

Greetings and profound respect

Toussaint L'Ouverture

18

ANTI-CORRUPTION PROCLAMATION

9 Thermidor, year 9 (29 July 1801)

As a public servant I must render justice without pay. Therefore, all acts on my part will be granted without charge to individuals [except for the issuing of passports]. No public functionary shall demand payment, in the name of his ministry, except those that have been authorized by the law or by regulations prior to this one.[1]

19

HAITIAN
CONSTITUTION OF 1801

Toussaint convoked an assembly to draft a constitution for St-Domingue on 4 February 1801. As with the reinterpretation of the rights of man and citizen that he had promoted since 1793, Toussaint here took strategic advantage of calls among French conservative forces to reintroduce 'special' laws for the colonies (traditionally a means of justifying slavery) to promote both the autonomy of the colony in a period of increasing reaction as well as his own personal hold on power. Members of this assembly included Julien Raimond (an emissary of Bonaparte to the colony) and the white planter and mayor of Port-au-Prince Bernard Borgella. The committee included not a single former slave. Completed in May, the constitution was promulgated in June 1801. The constitution reflects the many contradictions of L'Ouverture's political and social philosophy. On the one hand, it is the first modern constitution to address the conflict between the defence of property rights and human rights: if all humans possess a fundamental and inalienable freedom, property rights must logically be explicitly qualified not to include humans. Aside from Robespierre's never-adopted 1793 proposal for just such a constitutional limitation, this constitution was the first in Western modernity explicitly to base itself on the unlimited, universal right to freedom from enslavement. At the same time, the document puts in place a secondary series of paternalistic, authoritarian measures. If fully implemented, these would have so severely curtailed public freedom in every specific dimension as to regress far behind the various French constitutions – both pre- and post-Thermidor – the document draws from.[1]

The representatives of the colony of St-Domingue, gathered in Central Assembly, have identified and established the constitutional bases of the regime of the French colony of St-Domingue as follows:

TITLE I
OF THE TERRITORY

Art. 1. St-Domingue in its entire expanse, and Samana, La Tortue, La Gonave, Les Cayemites, L'Ile-a-Vache, La Saone and other adjacent islands form the territory of a single colony, which is part of the French Empire, but ruled under particular laws.

Art. 2. The territory of this colony is divided in departments, *arrondissements* (districts) and parishes.

TITLE II
OF THE INHABITANTS

Art. 3. There cannot exist slaves on this territory, servitude is therein forever abolished. All men are born, live and die free and French.[2]

Art. 4. All men, regardless of colour, are eligible for all employment.

Art. 5. There shall exist no distinction other than those based on virtue and talent, and other superiority afforded by law in the exercise of a public function.[3]

The law is the same for all whether in punishment or in protection.[4]

TITLE III
OF THE RELIGION

Art. 6. The Catholic, apostolic, Roman faith shall be the only publicly professed faith.[5]

Art. 7. Each parish shall provide for the maintenance of the cult of religion and of its ministers. The wealth of the factories shall be especially allocated to this expense, and the residences to the housing of ministers.

Art. 8. The Governor of the colony shall assign to each minister of religion the extent of his spiritual administration, and said ministers can never, under any circumstance, form a corps in the colony.

TITLE IV
OF THE MORES

Art. 9. Marriage, by its civic and religious institution, supports the purity of mores; spouses who will practise the virtues required by their condition shall always be distinguished and specially protected by the government.

Art. 10. Divorce shall not take place in the colony.

Art. 11. Laws that will tend to expand and maintain social virtues, and to encourage and cement family bonding, shall fix the condition and rights of children born in wedlock.

TITLE V
OF MEN IN SOCIETY

Art. 12. The Constitution guarantees freedom and individual security. No one shall be arrested unless by a formally expressed mandate, issued from a functionary to whom the law grants the right to order arrest and detention in a publicly designated location.

Art. 13. Property is sacred and inviolable. Each person, either by himself, or by his representatives, has the free right to dispose of and to administer property that is recognized as belonging to him. Anyone who attempts to deny this right shall become guilty of crime towards society and responsible towards the person whose property is troubled.[6]

TITLE VI
OF CULTURES AND COMMERCE

Art. 14. The colony being essentially agricultural cannot suffer the least disruption in the works of its cultivation.[7]

Art. 15. Each plantation shall constitute a manufacture that requires the gathering of cultivators and workers; it shall represent the quiet haven of an active and constant family, of which the owner of the land or his representative shall be the father.

Art. 16. Each cultivator and each worker is a member of the family and is entitled to a share in the revenues.

Every change in domicile on the part of the cultivator threatens the ruin of of the crops. In order to repress a vice as disruptive to the colony as it is to public order, the Governor issues all policy requirements necessary in the circumstances and in conformance with the bases of the rules of police of 20

Vendémiaire, year IX [12 October 1800], and of the proclamation of the following 19th Pluviôse [9 February 1801] of the Chief General Toussaint-L'Ouverture.

Art. 17. The introduction of cultivators indispensable to the re-establishment and to the growth of agriculture shall take place in St-Domingue. The Constitution charges the Governor to take convenient measures to encourage and favour the increase in manpower, to stipulate and balance the diverse interests, to ensure and guarantee the execution of respective engagements resulting from this process.

Art. 18. Commerce in the colony consists uniquely of exchange goods produced on its territory; consequently, the introduction of goods similar in nature is and shall remain prohibited.

TITLE VII
OF THE LEGISLATION AND LEGISLATIVE AUTHORITY

Art. 19. The colonial regime is determined by laws proposed by the Governor and rendered by a gathering of inhabitants, who shall meet at fixed periods at the central seat of the colony under the title Central Assembly of St-Domingue.[8]

Art. 20. No law relative to the internal administration of the colony shall be promulgated unless it contains the following formula:

The Central Assembly of St-Domingue, upon the proposition of the Governor, renders the following law:

Art. 21. No law shall be obligatory to the citizen until the day it is promulgated in the chief town of each department.

The promulgation of law shall take place as follows: In the name of the French colony of St-Domingue, the Governor orders that the subsequent law be sealed, promulgated and executed in all of the colony.

Art. 22. The Central Assembly of St-Domingue shall be composed of two representatives of each department, whom, to be eligible, shall be at least thirty years of age and have resided for five years in the colony.

Art. 23. The Assembly shall be renewed every two years by half; no one shall be a member for six consecutive years. The election shall proceed as follows: every two years each municipality nominates one deputy each, on the 10th Ventôse [1 March], each of the deputies, who shall meet ten days thereafter at the chief town of their respective departments, where they shall form as many departmental electoral assemblies that will each nominate one representative to the Central Assembly.

The next election shall take place on the 10th Ventôse of the eleventh year of the French Republic [1 March 1803]. In case of death, resignation or other vacancy of one or several members of the Assembly, the Governor shall provide a replacement.

He shall equally designate the members of the current Central Assembly who, at the time of its first renewal, shall remain members of the Assembly for two additional years.

Art. 24. The Central Assembly shall vote the adoption or the rejection of laws that are proposed to it by the Governor; it shall express its vote on rules made and on the application of laws already made, on abuses to correct, on improvements to undertake in all parts of service of the colony.

Art. 25. The session shall begin each year on the 1st Germinal (22 March) and shall not exceed three months in duration. The Governor can convoke the Assembly in extraordinary meeting; the hearings shall not be public.

Art. 26. On the state of revenues and spending that are proposed to the Assembly by the Governor, the Central Assembly shall determine, when appropriate, establishment of rates, quotas, the duration and mode of tax collection, its increase or decrease; these conditions shall be summarily printed.

TITLE VIII
OF THE GOVERNMENT

Art. 27. The administrative direction of the government shall be entrusted to a Governor who corresponds directly with the government of the Metropole, on all matters relative to the interests of the colony.

Art. 28. The Constitution nominates the citizen Toussaint-L'Ouverture, Chief General of the army of St-Domingue, and, in consideration for important services rendered to the colony, in the most critical circumstances of the revolution, and upon the wishes of the grateful inhabitants, he is entrusted the direction thereof for the remainder of his glorious life.[9]

Art. 29. In the future, each Governor shall be nominated for five years, and shall continue every five years for reasons of his good administration.

Art. 30. In order to strengthen the tranquillity that the colony owes to the steadfastness, activity, indefatigable zeal and rare virtues of General Toussaint L'Ouverture, and as a sign of the unlimited trust of the inhabitants of St-Domingue, the constitution attributes exclusively to this general the right to designate the citizen who, in the unfortunate event of the general's death, shall immediately replace him. This choice shall remain secret; it shall be cosigned under sealed envelope to be opened only by the Central Assembly, in the presence of all active generals and chief commanders of departments of the army of St-Domingue.

The Governor Toussaint L'Ouverture shall take all necessary precautionary measures to let the Central Assembly know the depository of this important envelope.

Art. 31. The citizen who shall be chosen by the Governor Toussaint L'Ouverture to take the leadership of the government upon his death, shall swear in front of the Central Assembly to execute the Constitution of St-Domingue and to remain attached to the French government, and shall be immediately installed in his functions; all this shall be done in the presence of the active generals and chief commanders of departments of the army of St-Domingue, who all, individually and without delay, shall swear obedience to the orders of the new Governor of St-Domingue.

Art. 32. At least one month before the expiration of the five years fixed for the administration of each Governor, the said Governor, jointly with the active-duty generals and chief commanders of departments, shall meet at the ordinary place of hearing of the Central Assembly, in order to nominate, concurrently with the members of this Assembly, the new Governor or to continue the administration of the one who is in place.

Art. 33. Failure of a Governor to convoke [the General Assembly] constitutes a manifest infraction of the Constitution. In such circumstance, the highest-ranked general or the senior general of equal rank, who is in active service in the colony, shall rightfully, if provisionally, take control of the government.

This general shall immediately convoke the other generals in active duty, the chief commanders of departments and the members of the Central Assembly, who shall all obey the convocation, in order to proceed concurrently to the nomination of a new Governor.

In the event of the death of, resignation of or other vacancy by a Governor before the expiration of his mandate, the position of Governor passes, again provisionally, to the highest-ranked general, or the senior general of equal rank who shall convoke, to the same ends as above, the members of the Central Assembly, the active-duty generals and the chief commanders of the departments.

Art. 34. The Governor shall seal and promulgate the laws; he nominates to all civilian and military employment. He is the chief commander of the armed forces and is charged with its organization; state vessels in station at the shores of the colony receive orders from him.

He shall determine the divisions of the territory most beneficial to internal relations. He watches and provides, according to the law, for the internal and external security of the colony, and given that the state of war is a state of abandonment, malaise and nullity for the colony, in those circumstances the Governor is charged to take measures he deems necessary to ensure the subsistence of and the supply of goods of all sorts to the colony.

Art. 35. He shall exercise the general policing of inhabitants and of the factories, and enforce the obligations of owners, farmers and their representatives towards cultivators and workers, and the duty of cultivators towards owners, farmers and their representatives.

Art. 36. He shall propose laws to the Central Assembly, as well as changes to the Constitution that experience may necessitate.

Art. 37. He shall direct and supervise the collection, the payments and the use of finances of the colony, and shall give, to this effect, any and all orders.

Art. 38. He shall present, every two years, to the Central Assembly the receipts and disbursements of each department, year by year.

Art. 39. He shall supervise and censor by the authority of his commissaries, all writings intended for printing on the island; he shall censor all those coming from abroad that would tend to corrupt mores or trouble the new colony; he shall punish the authors or bearers of these writings, according to the severity of the situation.

Art. 40. If the Governor is informed of some plot against the tranquillity of the colony, he shall immediately proceed to the arrest of the presumed authors, instigators or accomplices; after having them undergo extra-judicial questioning, he shall cite them in front of a competent tribunal.

Art. 41. The salary of the Governor is fixed at the present time at 300.000 francs. His honour guard shall be charged to the colony.

TITLE IX
OF THE COURTS

Art. 42. Citizens shall have an inalienable right to be tried by Judges [*arbitres*] if they so wish.

Art. 43. No authority shall suspend or impeach the execution of judgements rendered by the courts.

Art. 44. Justice shall be administered in the colony by courts of first instance and by courts of appeal. The law determines their organization, their number, their competence and the territory of each court's jurisdiction.

These tribunals, according to their jurisdiction, shall recognize all civil and criminal affairs.

Art. 45. There shall exist for the colony a Court of Cassation that shall pronounce on requests for the annulment of judgements rendered by appeal courts, and issue opinions and those complaints made against an entire tribunal. This court does not hear the facts of the cases, but overturns judgements rendered on procedures in which due process has been violated; or that contain some express contravention [infringement] of the law, and shall return the evidence of the trial to the tribunal in question.

Art. 46. Judges of the various courts maintain their position for life, unless they are found guilty of forfeiture. Commissioners of the government can be revoked.

Art. 47. Military misdemeanours shall be submitted to special tribunals and subject to special judgements.

These special courts also hear cases of theft, abduction, violation of domicle, murder, assassination, arson, rape, treason and mutiny.

The organization of these courts pertains to the Governor of the colony.

TITLE X

OF MUNICIPAL ADMINISTRATIONS

Art. 48. There shall be in each parish of the colony a municipal administration; where there is a court of first instance, the administrative body shall be composed of a mayor and four administrators.

The commissioner to the government near the tribunal shall hold without remuneration the functions of commissioner to the municipal administration.

In other parishes, municipal administrations shall be composed of a mayor and two administrators; a substitute commissioner to the responsible tribunal shall hold the function of commissioner to the municipality without remuneration.

Art. 49. Members of these municipal administrations shall be nominated for two years; their position can be renewed. Their nomination devolves to the Governor, who, from a list of at least sixteen individuals, presented by each municipal administration, chooses the persons most appropriate to manage the affairs of each parish.

Art. 50. The function of municipal administrators consists in the exercise of the simple policing of cities and towns, in the administration of taxes originating from revenues of factories and additional obligations of the parishes.

They are, in addition, charged with the keeping of records of births, marriages and deaths.

Art. 51. The mayors exert particular functions determined by law.

TITLE XI
OF THE ARMED FORCES

Art. 52. The Armed Forces are essentially obedient, they can never deliberate; they are at the disposition of the Governor who can mobilize them only to maintain public order, protection due to all citizens, and the defence of the colony.

Art. 53. They are divided into the paid colonial guard and the unpaid colonial guard.

Art. 54. The unpaid colonial guard shall not go outside the limits of its parish unless there is a case of imminent danger, and upon the order and the responsibility of the local military commander.

Outside of its parish it shall be compensated; and shall submit, in this case, to military discipline, and in all other cases it is only subject to the law.

Art. 55. The state police force of the colony shall be part of the Armed Forces; it shall be divided into a mounted force and a pedestrian force. The mounted force is instituted for the policing of the countryside; it has charge of the wealth of the colony.

The pedestrian force is instituted for the policing of cities and towns; it shall be at the charge of the city or town for which it performs services.

Art. 56. The army is recruited upon the request of the Governor to the Central Assembly, according to the mode established by law.

TITLE XII
OF FINANCES, OF SEQUESTERED AND VACANT ESTATES

Art. 57. The finances of the colony shall be composed of: (1) duties on imports, weights and measures; (2) duties on the rental value of city and town houses, and duties on manufactured goods, other than agriculture and salt marshes; (3) revenues from ferries and postal services; (4) fines and confiscated wrecks; (5) duties on the rescue of wrecked ships; revenue of colonial domains.

Art. 58. The proceeds from the sale of sequestered properties of absentee and represented owners becomes provisionally part of the public revenue of the colony and shall be applied to expenses of administration.

Circumstances shall determine the laws that should be made relative to outstanding public debt, and to the farming of sequestered property collected by the administration prior to the promulgation of the present law.

Art. 59. Funds originating from the sales of personal estates and from the sale of vacant inheritances in the colony under the French government since 1789, shall be placed in a designated coffer. These shall not be available, along with real estate gathered under colonial domains, until two years after the announcement of peace in the island, between France and the maritime powers; let it be understood that this deadline is only relative to successions whose five-year deadline fixed by the edict of 1781 has expired; and concerning those opened on or around the peace period, they shall not become available and unified until after seven years.

Art. 60. Foreign successors of French parents or foreign parents in France shall succeed them also in St-Domingue; they shall be allowed to enter into contracts, acquire and receive properties situated in the colony, and dispose of them in the same manner as the French by all means authorized by laws.

Art. 61. Laws shall determine the mode of collection of finances of sequestered and vacant estates.

Art. 62. A temporary accounting commission shall regulate and verify the revenue and disbursement accounts of the colony; this commission shall consist of three members, chosen and nominated by the Governor.

TITLE XIII
GENERAL DISPOSITIONS

Art. 63. The residence of any person shall constitute an inviolable abode. During night-time, no one shall have the right to enter therein unless in case of fire, flooding or upon request from within. During the day, authorities shall have access for a particular objective determined either by a law or by an order issued by a public authority.

Art. 64. For an act ordering the arrest of a person to be executed, it must

(1) formally express the motive of the arrest and the law in virtue of which it is ordered;

(2) be issued by a functionary whom the law formally empowers to do so;

(3) be presented to the person in the form of a copy of the warrant.

Art. 65. Anyone who, without the authority of the law to make an arrest, gives, signs, executes or causes to be executed the arrest of a person shall be guilty of the crime of arbitrary detention.

Art. 66. Any person shall have the right to address individual petitions to all constitutional authorities and especially to the Governor.

Art. 67. There cannot exist in the colony corporations or associations that are contrary to public order.

No citizen association shall constitute a civil organization [société populaire]. All seditious gatherings shall be dissolved immediately, first by way of verbal order and, if necessary, by armed force.

Art. 68. Any person may form particular establishments of education and instruction for the youth under the authorization and the supervision of municipal administrations.

Art. 69. The law supervises in particular all professions regarding public mores, public safety, health and wealth of citizens.

Art. 70. The law provides for awards to inventors of agricultural tools, and for the preservation of the exclusive ownership of their discoveries.

Art. 71. There shall exist in the colony uniformity of weights and measures.

Art. 72. There shall be given, by the Governor, in the name of the colony, awards to soldiers who have rendered exceptional services while fighting for the common defence.

Art. 73. Absentee owners, for whatever reason, conserve all their rights to properties belonging to them and situated in the colony; it suffices, to remove any sequestration that might have been imposed, to reintroduce their titles of ownership and, in default of title thereof, supplementary acts whose formula is determined by law. Exempt from this disposition are, nevertheless, those who might have been inscribed and maintained on the general list of emigrants of France; their properties shall continue, in this case, to be administered as colonial domains until their removal from the list.

Art. 74. The colony proclaims, as a guarantee of public law, that all leases of properties legally leased by the administration shall have their full effect, if the contracting parties prefer not to enter into agreement with owners or their representatives who would obtain the return of their sequestered goods.

Art. 75. It proclaims that agriculture, all production, all means of employment and all social order are founded upon on the respect of persons and of properties.

Art. 76. It proclaims that any citizen owes services to the land that nourishes him or in which he was born, for the maintenance of freedom, equality and property, whenever the law calls upon him to defend them.

Art. 77. The Chief General Toussaint L'Ouverture is and shall remain charged with sending the present Constitution to be sanctioned by the French government; nevertheless, and given the absence of laws, the urgency to overcome the present perilous situation, the necessity promptly to re-establish agriculture and the unanimous wishes pronounced by the inhabitants of St-Domingue, the Chief General is henceforth invited, in the name of public good, to proceed with its execution in all areas of the territory of the colony.

Made at Port Républicain, this 19th Floréal, year IX [10 May 1801] of the French Republic, one and indivisible.

Signed:
Borgella, President,
Raymond Collet Gaston Nogérée,
Lacour,
Roxas,
Munos,
Mancebo,
E. Viert, secretary
After having taken knowledge of the Constitution, I give it my approval. The invitation of the Central Assembly is for me an order; consequently, I shall pass it to the French government in order to obtain its sanction; as for its execution in the colony, the wish expressed by the Central Assembly shall be fulfilled as well and executed.
Given at Cap Français, this 14th Messidor, year IX [3 July 1801] of the French Republic, one and indivisible.
The General in Chief:
Signed: Toussaint L'Ouverture

20

LETTER FROM NAPOLEON TO TOUSSAINT

18 November 1801

This letter was presented to Toussaint at his plantation at Ennery on 8 February 1802, by his two sons, returned from their studies in France, and their tutor Coisnon. The letter had little chance of success, as it named Leclerc as Toussaint's superior officer. In fact, virtually every word of it was either false or highly ambiguous; Leclerc had explicit orders from Napoleon to capture and deport Toussaint and the entire black officer class with him, and to reinstate slavery as soon as possible.

Citizen General

The peace with England and all the European powers, which has established the Republic in the highest degree of power and grandeur, now allows the government to occupy itself with the colony of St-Domingue. We are sending there Citizen Leclerc, our brother-in-law, in his quality as General to serve as first magistrate of the colony. He is accompanied by a considerable force in order to ensure the respect of the sovereignty of the French people.

It is in these circumstances that we hope that you will prove to us, and to all of France, the sincerity of the sentiments that you have regularly expressed in the letters that you wrote to us.

We hold you in esteem, and we are happy to recognize and proclaim the great services that you have rendered the French people. If its banner flies over St-Domingue, it is to you and the brave blacks that this is owed.

Called by your talents and the force of circumstances to the leading position of command, you have done away with civil war, put a brake on persecution by several ferocious men, and returned to its place of honour the cult of God, from which everything emanates.

The constitution you made, while including many good things, contains some that are contrary to the dignity and sovereignty of the French people, of which St-Domingue forms only a portion.

The circumstances in which you found yourself, surrounded on all sides by enemies without the metropole being able to either assist or resupply you, rendered articles of that constitution legitimate that otherwise would not be. But today, when the circumstances have changed for the better, you should be the first to render homage to the sovereignty of the nation that counts you among its most illustrious citizens thanks to the services you have rendered it and by the talents and the force of character with which nature has graced you. A contrary conduct would be irreconcilable with the idea we have conceived of you. It would have you lose the many rights to recognition and the benefits of the republic, and would dig beneath your feet a precipice which, in swallowing you up, could contribute to the misfortune of those brave blacks whose courage we love, and whose rebellion we would, with difficulty, be obliged to be punished.

We have made known to your children and their tutor the sentiments that animate us. We are returning them to you.

Assist the General with your counsels, your influence and your talents. What could you wish for? Freedom for blacks? You know that in all the countries we've been we have given it to people who didn't have it. Consideration, honours, fortune? After the services you have rendered us, that you can yet render us, and the particular sentiments that we have for you, can you possibly be unsure about your fortune and the honours that await you?

And, General, think that if you are the first of your colour to have arrived at such a great power, and to have so distinguished himself for his bravery and military talents, you are also before God and ourselves principally responsible for the conduct of the people of St-Domingue.

If there are evil ones who say to the individuals of St-Domingue that we arrive to investigate what they did during the time of anarchy, assure them that we are informing ourselves only of their conduct in those circumstances, and that we are only investigating the past in order to learn of the traits that distinguished them in the war they carried out against the English and the Spaniards, who were our enemies.

Count without any reservation on our esteem, and conduct yourself as should one of the principal citizens of the greatest nation in the world.

The First Consul, Bonaparte

21

PROCLAMATION

25 November 1801

This document testifies to the dictatorial 'delirium' (Dubois) that overtook L'Ouverture in response to the series of rebellions of October 1801 that culminated in Toussaint's decision to execute his adoptive nephew Moïse, thought to have led the uprisings. Its call for identity cards and a punitive regime of chain gang labour are the culmination of the forcible militar-ization of agriculture he attempted to implement from 1796 to 1802. Fundamentally, the proclamation demonstrates L'Ouverture's tragic inability to perceive the fundamental incompatibility between this tota-litarian social model and the uncompromising call for general liberty he continued to defend until his death.

Cap Français, 4 Frimmaire [Frimaire], year X

Since the revolution, I have done all that depended upon me to return happiness to my country and to ensure liberty for my fellow citizens. Forced to combat internal and external enemies of the French Republic, I made war with courage, honour and loyalty. I have never strayed from the rules of justice with my enemies; as much as was in my power I sought to soften the horrors of war, to spare the blood of men . . . Often after victory I received as brothers those who, the day before, were under enemy flags. Through the overlooking of errors and faults I wanted to make even its most ardent enemies love the legitimate and sacred cause of liberty.

I constantly reminded my brothers in arms, generals and officers, that the ranks to which they had been raised were nothing but the reward for honour, bravery and irreproachable conduct. That the higher they were above their fellow citizens, the more irreproachable all their actions and words must be; that scandals caused by public men had consequences even more dire for society than those of simple citizens; that the ranks and functions they bore had not been given to them to serve only their ambition, but had as cause and goal the general good. [. . .]

It is up to officers to set a good example to their soldiers. Every captain should have the noble goal of having his company the best disciplined, the most cleanly attired, the best trained. He should think that the lapses of his soldiers reflect on him and believe himself lowered by the faults of those he commands. [. . .]

Having always regarded religion as the basis of all virtues and the foundation of the happiness of societies, in one of my proclamations, at the time of the war in the south, I laid out the obligations of fathers and mothers, their obligation to raise their children in the love and fear of God.

Nevertheless, how negligently fathers and mothers raise their children, especially in cities. They leave them in a state of idleness and in ignorance of their principal obligations. They seem to inspire in children contempt for agriculture, the first, the most honourable, and the most useful of all occupations.

Barely are they born than we see these same children with jewels and earrings, covered in rags, their clothing filthy, wounding the eyes of decency through their nudity. Thus they arrive at the age of twelve, without moral principles, without a skill, and with a taste for luxury and laziness as their only education. And since bad impressions are difficult to correct, it is certain beyond any doubt that they will be bad citizens, vagabonds, thieves. And if they are girls, then they are prostitutes all of them ready to follow the prompting of the first conspirator who will preach murder and pillage to them. It is upon such vile mothers and fathers, on students so dangerous, that the magistrates of the people must ceaselessly keep an open eye.

The same reproaches equally apply to cultivators on the plantations. Since the revolution, perverse men have told them that freedom is the right to remain idle and to follow only their whims. Such a doctrine could not help but be accepted by evil men, thieves and assassins. It is time to hit out at the hardened men who persist in such ideas.

As soon as a child can walk, he should be employed on the plantations according to his strength in some useful work, instead of being sent into the cities where, under the pretext of an education that he doesn't receive, he learns vice, to join the horde of vagabonds and women of ill repute, to trouble by his existence the repose of good citizens, and to terminate it in ignominy. Military commanders and magistrates must be inexorable with this class of men. Despite this, they must be forced to be useful to society upon which, without the most severe vigilance, they will be a plague.

Since the revolution, it is evident that the war has made perish many more men than women. In addition, many more of the latter, whose existence is based on libertinage, can be found in the cities. Entirely given over to concern for their attire, a result of their prostitution, they want to do absolutely nothing that is useful. It is they who harbour evil men, who live on the products of their crimes. It would be all to the honour of magistrates, generals and commandants to not leave a single one in the cities. The least negligence in this regard would render them worthy of public lack or esteem. [. . .]

As for domestics, each citizen should only have as many as are necessary for indispensable services. The persons in whose homes they reside should be the first overseers of their conduct and should not tolerate anything in their conduct contrary to good morals, submission and order. If they are thieves they should be denounced to military commandants so they can be punished in conformity with the law. And since under the new regime all labour deserves a salary, every salary demands work. Such is the invariable and firm will of the government.

An object worthy of attention is the surveillance of foreigners who arrive in the colony. Some among them, knowing only of the changes that have taken place through the reports of enemies of the new order of things, make statements that are all the more dangerous in that they are avidly listened to by those who, basing their hopes on the troubles, ask only for pretexts. Such straying must be severely punished. The carelessness of public functionaries in this regard will undermine the confidence of which they are in need and will cause them to be looked upon, and rightly so, as accomplices of the enemies of freedom!

The most holy of all institutions among men who live in society, that from which flows the greatest good, is marriage [. . .] Thus a wise government must always occupy itself with surrounding happy couples with honour, respect and veneration. It should only rest after having extirpated immorality to the last root. Military commanders, and especially public functionaries, are inexcusable when they publicly give themselves over to the scandal of vice. Those who, while having legitimate wives, allow concubines within their houses, or those who, not being married, live publicly with several women, are not worthy of command: they shall be dismissed.

Idleness is the source of all disorders, and if it is at all tolerated, I shall hold the military commanders responsible, persuaded that those who tolerate idleness and vagabonds are secret enemies of the government.

In keeping with his abilities, no one under any pretext is to be exempt from some task. Creole mothers and fathers who have children and properties should go there to live and work, to make their children work or to oversee their labour; and in moments of rest they should, either themselves or through instructors, teach them the precepts of our religion.

It is through these means that useful and respectable citizens will be formed, and we will distance forever from this colony the horrible events whose memory should never be effaced from our minds.

Consequently, I decree the following:

Any commander who during the recent conspiracy [the October rebellions, brutally repressed by Dessaline and Christophe under L'Ouverture's orders] had knowledge of the troubles which were to break out and who tolerated pillage and murder or who, able to prevent or block the revolt, allowed the law that declares that 'life, property and the asylum of every citizen are sacred and inviolable' to be broken, will be brought before a special tribunal and punished in conformity with the law of 10 August 1801. Any military commander who, by lack of foresight or negligence, has not stopped the disorders that have been committed will be discharged and punished with one year in prison. In consequence of this, a rigorous inquest will be carried out, according to which the government will pronounce on his destiny.

All generals and commanders of *arrondissements* and quarters who in the future neglect to take all necessary measures to prevent or block sedition will be brought before a special tribunal and punished in conformity with the law of 10 August 1801.

In case of troubles, or upon indication that such will break out, the National Guard of a quarter or *arrondissement* shall be under the orders of the military commanders upon their simple requisition. Any military commander who shall not have taken all the measures necessary to prevent troubles in his quarter, or the spreading of trouble from a quarter neighbouring that which he commands, and any military man, be he of the line or the

National Guard, who shall refuse to obey legal orders shall be punished with death.

Any individual, man or woman, whatever his or her colour, who shall be convicted of having pronounced serious statements tending to incite sedition shall be brought before a court martial and punished in conformity with the law.

Any Creole individual, man or woman, convicted of making statements tending to alter public tranquillity but who shall not be worthy of death shall be sent to the fields to work with a chain on one foot for six months.

Any foreign individual found in the case of the preceding article shall be deported from the colony.

In all the communes of the colony where municipal administrations exist, all male and female citizens who live in them, whatever their quality or condition, must obtain a security card. Such card shall contain the name, family name, address, civil state, profession and quality, age and sex of the person who bears it. It shall be signed by the mayor and the police superintendent of the quarter in which lives the individual to which it shall be delivered. It shall be renewed every six months and paid at the price of one *gourdin* for each individual, and the sums coming from this are destined for communal expenses.

It is expressly ordered that municipal administrators are only to deliver security cards to persons having a known profession or state, irreproachable conduct and well-assured means of existence. All those who cannot fulfil the conditions rigorously necessary to obtain a security card will be sent to the fields if they are Creole, or sent away from the colony if they are foreigners.

Two weeks after the publication of the present act, any person found without a security card shall be sent to the fields if they are Creole and if they are foreigners deported from the colony without any form of trial if they don't prefer to serve in the troops of the line.

Any domestic who has not been judged worthy of obtaining a certificate of good conduct upon leaving a house in which he or she served shall be declared incapable of receiving a security card. Any person who, in order to favour them shall have delivered them one shall be punished with one month in prison.

Dating two weeks after the publication of the present act, all managers and drivers on plantations are to send to the commanders of their quarter the exact list of all the cultivators on their plantations of every age and sex, under penalty of one week in prison. Every manager and driver is the first overseer of his plantation. He is declared personally responsible for any kind of disorder that shall be committed, and for the laziness and vagabondage of the cultivators.

Dating from one month after the publication of the present act, all commanders of quarters are to send lists of the cultivators of all the plantations of their quarter to the *arrondissement* commanders under penalty of discharge.

The *arrondissement* commanders are to send list of all the plantations of their *arrondissements* to the generals under whose orders they serve, and these latter to the Governor as quickly as possible, under penalty of disobedience. Said lists, deposited in the archives of the government, shall serve in the future as the immutable bases for the fixing of cultivators on the plantations.

Any manager or driver of a plantation upon which a foreign cultivator shall have taken refuge shall denounce him to the captain or commander of the section within twenty-four hours under penalty of one week in prison.

Any captain or commander of a section who through negligence allowed a foreign cultivator on a plantation in his section for more than three days shall be discharged.

Vagabond cultivators arrested in this way shall be taken to the commander of the quarter, who will have them sent to the gendarmerie on their plantation. They will be confided to the special surveillance of the drivers and managers and they shall be deprived of passports for leaving the plantation for three months.

It is forbidden for any soldier to work on a plantation or for private individuals in the cities. Those who want to work and who obtain the permission of their officers shall be employed in labours for the account of the republic and paid according to their work.

It is forbidden for any soldier to go to a plantation, unless it is to see his father or mother and with a limited permit from his chief. If he fails to return to his corps at the stated hour he shall be punished in accordance with military ordinances.

Any person convicted of having disturbed or attempted to disturb a married couple shall be denounced to the civil and military authorities, who shall render an account to the Governor, who shall pronounce on their fate in accordance with the needs of the case.

My regulations on cultivation, given at Port Républicain on the 20th of Vendémiaire of the year IX [1800] shall be executed exactly as stated. All military commanders are enjoined to execute them rigorously and literally in all that is not contrary to the present proclamation.

The present proclamation shall be printed, transcribed on the registers of administrative and judiciary bodies, read, published and posted wherever needed, and also inserted in the *Bulletin Officiel de St-Domingue*. A copy shall be sent to all ministers of religion for it to be read to all parishioners after Mass.

All generals, military commanders and all civil authorities in all departments are enjoined to maintain a firm hand in ensuring the full and complete execution of all of these dispositions on their personal responsibility and under penalty of disobedience.

22

NAPOLEON'S ANALYSIS OF TOUSSAINT FROM ST HELENA

This fascinating text makes clear that the tragedy of the Haitian Revolution lay in part in the inability of these two leaders to overcome their own respective hubris: while Toussaint was unable to restrain himself from promulgating his constitution, though he was conscious that it would probably lead to open war with the French, Napoleon here reveals that he failed to follow his own better instincts, and in the process ended up losing virtually the entire French holdings in the Americas.

The prosperous situation in which the Republic found itself in 1801, after the Peace of Lunéville, made already foreseeable the moment when England would be obliged to lay down her arms, and when we would be empowered to adopt a definitive policy on St-Domingue. Two such options presented themselves to the meditations of the First Consul: the first to clothe General Toussaint L'Ouverture with civilian and military authority and with the title of Governor-General; to entrust command to the black generals; to consolidate and legalize the work discipline established by Toussaint, which had already been crowned by happy success; to require the black leaseholders [those who were operating the plantations of French colonists who had fled St-Domingue] to pay a tax or a rent to the former French proprietors, to conserve for the metropole the exclusive right to trade with the whole colony, by having the coasts patrolled by numerous cruisers. The other policy consisted of re-conquering the colony by force of arms, bringing back to France all the blacks who had occupied ranks superior to that of battalion chief, disarming the blacks while assuring them of their civil liberty, and restoring property to the [white] colonists. These projects each had advantages and inconveniences. The advantages of the first were palpable: the Republic would have an army of between 25,000 and 30,000 blacks, sufficient to make all America tremble; that would be a new element of power, and one that would cost no sacrifice, either in men or in money. The former landowners would doubtless lose three-quarters of their fortune; but French commerce would lose nothing there, since it always enjoyed exclusive trade privileges. The second project was more advantageous to the colonial landowners, [and] more in line with justice; but it required a war which would bring about the loss of many men and much money; the conflicting pretensions of the blacks, the coloured men and the white landowners would always be an object of discord and an embarrassment to the metropole; St-Domingue would always rest on a volcano: thus the First Consul was inclined towards the first policy, because that was the one that sound politics seemed to recommend to him – the one that would give more influence to his flag in America. What might he not undertake, with an army of the 25,000 to 30,000 blacks, in Jamaica, the Antilles, Canada, the United States even, and the Spanish colonies?

23

LETTER TO DESSALINES

8 February 1802

This letter, written just after the French troops under Leclerc landed in Le Cap on 4 February, describes the strategy of guerrilla warfare that would eventually carry the colony to independence and victory over the greatest army in the contemporary world. Already on that earlier date, Henry Christophe had inaugurated this scorched-earth policy by setting fire to Le Cap. General liberty was for the blacks of St-Domingue – as it was for their less successful colleagues Louis Delgrès and Joseph Ignace in Guadeloupe – a non-negotiable principle. In the name of general liberty and the unconditional refusal to be enslaved, all must be sacrificed without reserve.

LIBERTY. EQUALITY.

The Governor-General [Toussaint L'Ouverture] to General Dessalines, Commander-in-Chief of the army of the west

Headquarters Gonaïves, 8 February 1802

There is no reason for despair, Citizen-General, if you can succeed in removing from the [French] troops that have landed the resources offered to them by Port Républicain [Port-au-

Prince]. Endeavour, by all the means of force and address, to set that place on fire; it is constructed entirely of wood; you have only to send into it some faithful emissaries. Are there none under your orders devoted enough for this service? Ah! my dear General, what a misfortune that there was a traitor in that city, and that your orders and mine were not put into execution.

Watch for the moment when the garrison shall be weak in consequence of expeditions into the plains, and then try to surprise and carry that city, falling on it in the rear.

Do not forget, while waiting for the rainy season which will rid us of our foes, that we have no other resource than destruction and flames. Bear in mind that the soil bathed with our sweat must not furnish our enemies with the smallest aliment. Tear up the roads with shot; throw corpses and horses into all the fountains; burn and annihilate everything, in order that those who have come to reduce us to slavery may have before their eyes the image of that hell which they deserve.

Salutation and Friendship,
Toussaint L'Ouverture

24

LETTER TO NAPOLEON FROM ON BOARD THE *HEROS*

12 July 1802

This letter was written to Napoleon following Toussaint's capture by Leclerc's troops. Various interpretations have been offered for Toussaint's failure to foresee this betrayal, from hubris to complacency and world-weary fatigue, to a premonition that his self-sacrifice would galvanize a fragmented black and mulatto community to defeat the French invaders (an interpretation most eloquently articulated by Aimé Césaire). Whatever Toussaint's subjective state and motivations, it is clear that the latter effect was the objective result of his arrest and deportation to Fort de Joux.

1 Thermidor, year X

General Toussaint L'Ouverture to General Bonaparte, First Consul of the French Republic

Citizen First Consul

I will not conceal my faults from you. I have committed some. What man is exempt? I am quite ready to avow them. After the word of honour of the Captain-General [General Leclerc] who represents the French government, after a proclamation addressed to the colony, in which he promised to throw the veil of oblivion over the events that had taken place in St-Domingue, I, as you did on the Eighteenth Brumaire, withdrew into the bosom of my family. Scarcely had a month passed away, when evil-disposed persons, by means of intrigues, effected my ruin with the General-in-Chief, by filling his mind with distrust against me. I received a letter from him which ordered me to act in conjunction with General Brunet. I obeyed. Accompanied by two persons, I went to Gonaïves, where I was arrested. They sent me on board the frigate *Creole*, I know not for what reason, without any other clothes than those I had on. The next day my house was exposed to pillage; my wife and my children were arrested; they had nothing, not even the means to cover themselves.

Citizen First Consul: A mother fifty years of age may deserve the indulgence and the kindness of a generous and liberal nation. She has no account to render. I alone ought to be responsible for my conduct to the government I have served. I have too high an idea of the greatness and the justice of the First Magistrate of the French people, to doubt a moment of its impartiality. I indulge the feeling that the balance in its hands will not incline to one side more than to another. I claim its generosity.

Salutation and respect,
Toussaint L'Ouverture

25

LETTER TO NAPOLEON FROM FORT DE JOUX

17 September 1802

In the dungeon of Fort de Joux, this 30 Fructidor, year XI

General and First Consul

The respect and the submission which I could wish forever graven on my heart [here several words are illegible]. If I have sinned in doing my duty, it is contrary to my intentions; if I was wrong in forming the constitution, it was through my great desire to do good; it was through having employed too much zeal, too much self-love, thinking I was pleasing the government under which I served; if the formalities which I ought to have observed were neglected, it was through inattention. I have had the misfortune to incur your wrath, but as to fidelity and probity, I am strong in my conscience, and I dare affirm that among all the servants of the state no one is more honest than myself. I was one of your soldiers, and the first servant of the Republic in St-Domingue; but now I am wretched, ruined, dishonoured, a victim of my own services; let your sensibility be moved at my position. You are too great in feeling and too just not to pronounce a judgement as to my destiny. I charge General

Cafarelli, your aide-de-camp, to put my report into your hands. I beg you to take it into your best consideration. His honour and his frankness have forced me to open my heart to him.

Salutation and respect,
Toussaint L'Ouverture

26

MEMOIR OF
TOUSSAINT L'OUVERTURE

This text was first published in Paris in 1853 by the exiled Haitian lawyer Joseph Saint-Remy. Toussaint composed its seventy-five pages with the aid of a French secretary in his prison cell at the Fort de Joux in the Jura mountains, where he had arrived on 23 August 1802. Bonaparte never replied to L'Ouverture's entreaties, and by the following April the latter would die from the harsh conditions of his imprisonment. The text takes the form of a juridical brief for a military trial that would never occur. In it, the leading architect of the Haitian Revolution argues that the devastation of the island and the deaths of some 20,000 French troops were due entirely to General Leclerc's breaches of military protocol. Though the document is a first-hand account, it must be read critically, since Toussaint seeks to present his own participation in the most favourable light. Moreover, Toussaint was unaware, though he most likely suspected, that his capturer Leclerc had arrived in St-Domingue with explicit orders from Napoleon to reinstate slavery. He further ordered Leclerc to 'arrest [. . .] all the black generals' and 'not [to] allow any blacks having held a rank above that of captain to remain on the island'.[1]

It is my duty to render to the French government an exact account of my conduct. I shall relate the facts with all the simplicity and frankness of an old soldier, adding to them the reflections that naturally suggest themselves. In short, I shall tell the truth, though it be against myself.

The colony of St-Domingue, of which I was commander, enjoyed the greatest tranquillity; agriculture and commerce flourished there. The island had attained a degree of splendour that it had never before seen. And all this – I dare to say it – was my work.

Nevertheless, as we were upon a war footing, the Commission had published a decree ordering me to take all necessary measures to prevent the enemies of the Republic from penetrating into the island. Accordingly, I ordered all the commanders of the seaports not to permit any ships of war to enter into the roadstead, unless they were known and had obtained permission from me. If it should be a squadron, no matter from what nation, it was absolutely prohibited from entering the port, or even the road-stead, unless I should myself know where it came from, and the port from which it sailed.

This order was in force when, on 26 January 1802, a squadron appeared before Cap Français [Cap Haïtien]. At that time I had left this town to visit the Spanish part, Santo Domingo, for the purpose of inspecting the agriculture. On setting out from Maguâna, I had despatched one of my aides-de-camp to Gen. Dessalines, commander-in-chief of the departments of the West and South, who was then at St-Marc, to order him to join me at Gonaïves, or at St-Michel, to accompany me on my journey.

At the time of the squadron's appearance, I was in Santo Domingo, from which place I set out, three days after, to go to Hinche. Passing by Banique, arriving at Papayes, I met my aide-de-camp Couppé and an officer sent by Gen. Christophe, who brought me a letter from the general, by which he informed me of the arrival of the French squadron before the Cap, and assured me that the general-in-chief commanding this squadron had not done him the honour to write to him, but had only sent an officer to order him to prepare accommodations for his forces; that Gen. Christophe having demanded of this officer whether he was the bearer of a letter to him or of dispatches for the General-in-Chief, Toussaint L'Ouverture, requesting him to send them to him, that they might reach him at once, this officer replied to him that he was not charged with any, and that it was not, in fact, a question concerning Gen. Toussaint. 'Surrender the town,' he continued; 'you will be well recompensed; the French government sends you presents.' To which Gen. Christophe replied, 'Since you have no letters for the General-in-Chief nor for me, you may return and tell your general that he does not know his duty; that it is not thus that people present themselves in a country belonging to France.'

Gen. Leclerc, having received this answer, summoned Gen. Christophe to deliver the place to him, and, in case of refusal, warned him that on the morning of the next day he should land fifteen thousand men. In response to this, Gen. Christophe begged him to wait for Gen. Toussaint L'Ouverture, to whom he had already sent the intelligence, and would do so a second time without delay. In fact, I received a second letter, and hastened to reach the Cap, in spite of the overflowing of the Hinche, hoping to have the pleasure of embracing my brothers-in-arms from Europe, and to receive at the same time the orders of the French government; and in order to march with greater speed, I left all my escorts. Between St-Michel and St-Raphaël, I met Gen. Dessalines and said to him, 'I have sent for you to accompany me on my tour to Port-de-Paix, and to Môle; but that is useless now. I have just received two letters from Gen. Christophe, announcing the arrival of the French squadron before the Cap.'

I communicated to him these letters, whereupon he told me that he had seen from St-Marc six large vessels making sail for the coast of Port Républicain [Port-au-Prince]; but he did not know to which nation they belonged. I ordered him then to repair promptly to this port, since it was possible that Gen. Christophe having refused the entrance to the Cap to the general commanding the squadron, the latter might have proceeded to Port Républicain in the hope of finding me there; should this prove true, I ordered him in advance to request the general to wait for me, and to assure him that I would go first to the Cap in the hope of meeting him there, and in case I should not find him there, I would repair at once to Port Républicain to confer with him. I set out for the Cap, passing by Vases, the shortest road. On arriving upon the heights of the Grand Boucan, in the place called the Porte-Saint-Jacques, I perceived a fire in the city of Cap Français. I urged my horse at full speed to reach this town, to find there the general commanding the squadron, and to ascertain who had caused the conflagration. But, on approaching, I found the roads filled with the inhabitants who had fled from this unfortunate town, and I was unable to penetrate farther because all the passages were cannonaded by the artillery of the vessels which were in the roadstead. I then resolved to go up to the Fort of Bel-Air, but I found this fort evacuated likewise, and all the pieces of cannon spiked.

I was, consequently, obliged to retrace my steps. After passing the hospital, I met Gen. Christophe, and asked him who had ordered the town to be fired. He replied that it was he. I reprimanded him severely for having employed such rigorous measures. 'Why,' said I to him, 'did you not rather make some military arrangements to defend the town until my arrival?' He answered, 'What do you wish, general? My duty, necessity, the circumstances, the reiterated threats of the general commanding the squadron, forced me to it. I showed the general the orders of which I was the bearer, but without avail.' He added that the proclamations spread secretly in the town to seduce the people, and instigate an uprising, were not sanctioned by military usage;

that if the commander of the squadron had truly pacific intentions, he would have waited for me; that he would not have employed the means which he used to subdue the commander of Fort Boque, who is a drunkard; that he would not in consequence have seized this fort; that he would not have put to death half of the garrison of Fort Liberty; that he would not have made a descent upon Acul, and that, in a word, he would not have committed all the hostilities of which he was guilty.

Gen. Christophe joined me, and we continued the route together. On arriving at Haut-du-Cap, we passed through the Bréda plantation[2] as far as the barrier of Boulard, passing by the gardens. There I ordered him to rally his troops, and go into camp on the Bonnet until further orders, and to keep me informed of all the movements he made. I told him that I was going to Héricourt; that there, perhaps, I should receive news from the commander of the squadron; that he would doubtless deliver to me the orders of the government; that I might even meet him there; that I should then ascertain the reasons which had induced him to come in this manner; and, that, in case he was the bearer of orders from the government, I should request him to communicate them to me, and should in consequence make arrangements with him.

Gen. Christophe left me then to repair to the post which I had assigned to him; but he met a body of troops who fired upon him, forced him to dismount from his horse, plunge into the river, and cross it by swimming.

After separating from Gen. Christophe, I had at my side Adjutant-General Fontaine, two other officers, and my aide-de-camp, Couppé, who went in advance; he warned me of the troops on the road. I ordered him to go forward. He told me that this force was commanded by a general. I then demanded a conference with him. But Couppé had not time to execute my orders; they fired upon us at twenty-five steps from the barrier. My horse was pierced with a ball; another ball carried away the hat of one of my officers. This un-expected circumstance forced me to abandon the open road, to cross the savannah and the forests to reach Héricourt, where I remained three days to wait for news of the commander of the squadron, again without avail.

But, the next day, I received a letter from Gen. Rochambeau, announcing 'that the column which he commanded had seized Fort Liberty, taken and put to the sword a part of the garrison, which had resisted; that he had not believed the garrison would steep its bayonets in the blood of Frenchmen; on the contrary, he had expected to find it disposed in his favour'. I replied to this letter, and, manifesting my indignation to the general, asked to know, 'Why he had ordered the massacre of those brave soldiers who had only followed the orders given them; who had, besides, contributed so much to the happiness of the colony and to the triumph of the Republic. Was this the recompense that the French government had promised them?'

I concluded by saying to Gen. Rochambeau that 'I would fight to the last to avenge the death of these brave soldiers, for my own liberty, and to re-establish tranquillity and order in the colony.'

This was, in fact, the resolution I had taken after having reflected deliberately upon the report Gen. Christophe had brought me, upon the danger I had just run, upon the letter of Gen. Rochambeau, and finally upon the conduct of the commander of the squadron.

Having formed my resolution, I went to Gonaïves. There I communicated my intentions to Gen. Maurepas, and ordered him to make the most vigorous resistance to all vessels which should appear before Port-de-Paix, where he commanded; and, in case he should not be strong enough – having only half of a brigade – to imitate the example of Gen. Christophe and afterward withdraw to the mountain, taking with him ammuni-tion of all kinds; there to defend himself to the death.

I then went to St-Marc to visit the fortifications. I found that the news of the shameful events which had just taken place had reached this town, and the inhabitants had already fled. I gave orders for all the resistance to be made that the fortifications and munitions would allow of.

As I was on the point of setting out from this town to go to Port-au-Prince and the southern part to give my orders, captains Jean-Philippe Dupin and Isaac brought me dispatches from Paul L'Ouverture, who commanded at Santo Domingo. Both informed me that a descent had just been made upon Oyarsaval, and that the French and Spaniards who inhabited this place had risen and cut off the roads from Santo Domingo. I acquainted myself with these dispatches. In running over the letter of Gen. Paul and the copy of Gen. Kerverseau's to the commander of the place of Santo Domingo, which was enclosed in it, I saw that this general had made an overture to the commander of the place, and not to Gen. Paul, as he should have done, to make preparations for the landing of his force. I also saw the refusal given by Gen. Paul to this invitation, until he should receive orders from me. I replied to Gen. Paul that I approved his conduct, and ordered him to make all possible efforts to defend himself in case of attack; and even to make prisoners of Gen. Kerverseau and his force, if he could. I returned my reply by the captains just mentioned. But foreseeing, on account of the interception of the roads, that they might be arrested and their dispatches demanded, I gave them in charge a second letter, in which I ordered Gen. Paul to use all possible means of conciliation with Gen. Kerverseau. I charged the captains, in case they should be arrested, to conceal the first letter and show only the second.

My reply not arriving as soon as he expected, Gen. Paul sent another black officer with the same dispatches in duplicate. I gave only a receipt to this officer, and sent him back. Of these three messengers two were black and the other white. They were arrested, as I had anticipated; the two blacks were assassinated in violation of all justice and right, contrary to the customs of war; their dispatches were sent to Gen. Kerverseau, who concealed the first letter and showed to Gen. Paul only the second, in which I had ordered him to enter into negotiations with Gen. Kerverseau. It was in consequence of this letter that Santo Domingo was surrendered.

Having sent off these dispatches, I resumed my route towards the south. I had hardly set forward when I was overtaken by an orderly, coming up at full speed, who brought me a package from Gen. Vernet and a letter from my wife, both announcing to me the arrival from Paris of my two children and their preceptor, of which I was not before aware. I learned also that they were bearers of orders for me from the First Consul. I retraced my steps and flew to Ennery, where I found my two children and the excellent tutor whom the First Consul had had the goodness to give them. I embraced them with the greatest satisfaction and ardour. I then enquired if they were bearers of letters from the First Consul for me. The tutor replied in the affirmative, and handed me a letter which I opened and read about half through; then I folded it, saying that I would reserve the reading of it for a more quiet moment. I begged him then to impart to me the intentions of the government, and to tell me the name of the commander of the squadron, which I had not yet been able to ascertain. He answered, that his name was Leclerc; that the intention of the government towards me was very favourable, which was confirmed by my children, and of which I afterwards assured myself by finishing the letter of the First Consul. I observed to them, nevertheless, that if the intentions of the government were pacific and good regarding me and those who had contributed to the happiness which the colony enjoyed, Gen. Leclerc surely had not followed nor executed the orders he had received, since he had landed on the island like an enemy, and done evil merely for the pleasure of doing it, without addressing himself to the commander or making known to him his powers. I then asked Citizen Coisnon, my children's tutor, if Gen. Leclerc had not given him a dispatch for me or charged him with something to tell me. He replied in the negative, advising me, however, to go to the Cap to confer with the general; my children added their solicitations to persuade me to do so. I represented to them, 'that, after the conduct of this general, I could have no confidence in him; that he had landed like an enemy; that, in spite of that, I had believed it my duty to go to meet him in order to prevent the progress of the evil; that he had fired upon me, and I had run the greatest dangers; that, in short, if his intentions were as pure as those of the government which sent him, he should have taken the trouble to write to me to inform me of his mission; that, before arriving in the roadstead, he should have sent me an advice-boat with you, sir, and my children – that being the ordinary practice – to announce their arrival, and to impart to me his powers; that, since he had observed none of these formalities, the evil was done, and therefore I should refuse decidedly to go in search of him; that, nevertheless, to prove my attachment and submission to the French government, I would consent to write a letter to Gen. Leclerc. I shall send to him,' I continued, 'by Mr Granville, a worthy man, accompanied by my two children and their tutor, whom I shall charge to say to Gen. Leclerc, that it is absolutely dependent upon himself whether this colony is entirely lost, or preserved to France; that I will enter into all possible arrangements with him; that I am ready to submit to the orders of the French government; but that Gen. Leclerc shall show me orders of which he is. bearer, and shall, above all, cease from every species of hostility.'

In fact, I wrote the letter, and the deputation set out. In the hope that after the desire I had just manifested to render my submission, order would again be restored, I remained at Gonaïves till the next day. There I learned that two vessels had attacked St-Marc; I proceeded there and learned that they had been repulsed. I returned then to Gonaïves to wait for Gen. Leclerc's reply. Finally, two days after, my two children arrived with the response so much desired, by which the general commanded me to report in person to him, at the Cap, and announced that he had furthermore ordered his generals to advance upon all points; that his orders being given, he could not revoke them. He promised, however, that Gen. Boudet should be stopped at Artibonite; I concluded then, that he did not know the country perfectly, or had been deceived; for, in order to reach Artibonite, it was necessary to have a free passage by St-Marc, which was impossible now, since the two vessels which had attacked this place had been repulsed. He added, further, that they should not attack Môle, only blockade it, since this place had already surrendered. I replied then plainly to the general, 'that I should not report to him at the Cape; that his conduct did not inspire me with sufficient confidence; that I was ready to deliver the command to him in conformity with the orders of the First Consul, but that I would not be his lieutenant-general'. I besought him again to let me know his intentions, assuring him that I would contribute everything in my power to the re-establishment of order and tranquillity. I added, in conclusion, that if he persisted in his invasion, he would force me to defend myself, although I had but few troops. I sent him this letter with the utmost despatch, by an orderly, who brought me back word, 'that he had no reply to make and had taken the field'.

The inhabitants of Gonaïves then asked my permission to send a deputation to Gen. Leclerc, which I accorded to them, but he retained the deputation.

The next day I learned that he had taken, without striking a blow and without firing a gun, Dondon, St-Raphaël, St-Michel and Marmelade, and that he was prepared to march against Ennery and Gonaïves.

These new hostilities gave rise to new reflections. I thought that the conduct of Gen. Leclerc was entirely contrary to the intentions of the government, since the First Consul, in his letter, promised peace, while the general made war. I saw that, instead of seeking to arrest this evil, he only increased it. 'Does he not fear,' I said to myself, 'in pursuing such conduct, to be blamed by his government? Can he hope to be approved by the First Consul, that great man whose equity and impartiality are so well known, while I shall be disapproved?' I resolved then to defend myself, in case of attack; and in spite of my few troops, I made my dispositions accordingly.

Gonaïves not being defensible, I ordered it to be burned, in case retreat was necessary. I placed Gen. Christophe, who had been obliged to fall back, in the Eribourg road, which leads to Bayonnet, and withdrew myself to Ennery, where a part of my guard of honour had repaired to join and defend me. There I learned that Gros-Morne had just surrendered, and that the army was to march against Gonaïves with three columns; one of these, commanded by Gen. Rochambeau, intending to pass by Couleuvre and come down upon La Croix, to cut off the road from the town and the passage of the bridge of Ester.

I ordered Gonaïves to be burned, and, ignorant of Gen. Rochambeau's strength, marched to meet the column, which was making for the bridge of Ester, at the head of three hundred grenadiers of my guard, commanded by their chief, and of sixty mounted guards. We met in a gorge. The attack commenced at six o'clock in the morning with a continuous fire which lasted until noon. Gen. Rochambeau began the attack. I learned from the prisoners I took that the column numbered more than four thousand men. While I was engaged with Gen. Rochambeau, the column commanded by Gen. Leclerc reached Gonaïves.

After the engagement at La Croix, I proceeded to the bridge of Ester, with artillery, to defend the place, intending to go thence to St-Marc, where I expected to make a desperate resistance. But, on setting out, I learned that Gen. Dessalines, having arrived at this place before me, was obliged to evacuate it and retire to Petite Rivière. I was obliged, after this manoeuvre, to slacken my march in order to send in advance the prisoners taken at La Croix, and the wounded to Petite Rivière; and I determined to proceed there myself. When we reached Couriotte, in the plain, I left my troops there, and went in advance alone. I found all the country abandoned.

I received a letter from Gen. Dessalines, informing me that, having learned that the Cahos was to be attacked, he had gone to defend it. I sent an order to him to join me at once. I ordered the ammunition and provisions which I had with me to be put in Fort L'Ouverture at the Crête-à-Pierrot. I ordered Gen. Vernet to procure vessels which would contain water enough to last the garrison during a siege. On the arrival of Gen. Dessalines, I ordered him to take command of the fort and defend it to the last extremity.

For this purpose I left him half of my guards with the chief-of-brigade, Magny, and my two squadrons. I charged him not to allow Gen. Vernet to be exposed to fire, but to let him remain in a safe place to superintend the making of cartridges. Finally, I told Gen. Dessalines that while Gen. Leclerc was attacking this place, I should go into the northern part, make a diversion, and retake the different places which had been seized; by this manoeuvre, I should force the general to retrace his steps and make arrangements with me to preserve this beautiful colony to the government.

Having given these orders, I took six companies of grenadiers commanded by Gabart, chief of the fourth demi-brigade, and Pourcely, the chief-of-battalion, and marched upon Ennery. I found there a proclamation of Gen. Leclerc, pronouncing me an outlaw. Confident that I had done no wrong with which to reproach myself, that all the disorder that prevailed in the country had been occasioned by Gen. Leclerc; believing myself, besides, the legitimate commander of the island – I refuted his proclamation and declared him to be outlawed. I immediately resumed my march and recaptured, without violence, St-Michel, St-Raphaël, Dondon and Marmelade. In this last place I received a letter from Gen. Dessalines, announcing that Gen. Leclerc had marched against Petite Rivière with three columns; that one of these columns, passing by Cahos and Grand Fonds, had captured all the treasures of the Republic coming from Gonaïves, and some silver which the inhabitants had deposited; that it was so heavily loaded with booty it was unable to reach its destination, and had been obliged to turn back to deposit its riches at Port Républicain; that the two other columns, which had attacked the fort, had been repulsed by the chief-of-brigade, Magny; that Gen. Leclerc, having united his forces, had ordered a second attack, which had likewise been repelled by himself, Dessalines, who had then arrived. Apprised of these facts, I moved upon Plaisance and captured the camp of Bidouret, who held this place. This camp was occupied by troops of the line. I assaulted all the advanced posts at the same time. Just as I was going to fall upon Plaisance, I received a letter from the commander of Marmelade, which gave me notice that a strong column from the Spanish part was advancing upon this latter place.

I then moved promptly upon this column, which, instead of advancing upon Marmelade, had marched upon Hinche, where I pursued, but was unable to overtake it. I returned to Gonaïves, made myself master of the plain surrounding the town, ready to march upon the Gros-Morne to support Gen. Maurepas, whom I supposed must be at Port-de-Paix, or else retired to the mountains where I ordered him to encamp, not knowing that he had already capitulated and submitted to Gen. Leclerc.

I received a third letter from Gen. Dessalines, who reported that Gen. Leclerc, having ordered a general assault and been repulsed, had determined to surround the place and bombard it. As soon as I learned the danger with which he was threatened, I hastened to move my troops there to deliver him. Arrived before the camp, I made a reconnaissance, procured the necessary information and prepared to attack it. I could, without fail, have entered the camp by a weak side which I had discovered, and seized the person of Gen. Leclerc and all his staff; but at the moment of execution I received information that the garrison, failing of water, had been obliged to evacuate the fort. If the project had succeeded, my intention was to send Gen. Leclerc back to the First Consul, rendering to him an exact account of his conduct, and praying him to send me another person worthy of his confidence, to whom I could deliver up the command.

I retired to Grand Fonds to wait for the garrison of Crête-à-Pierrot and to unite my forces. As soon as the garrison arrived, I enquired of Gen. Dessalines where the prisoners were whom he had previously told me were at Cahos. He replied that a part had been taken by Gen. Rochambeau's column, that another part had been killed in the different attacks that he had endured, and that the rest had escaped in the various marches which he had been obliged to make. This reply shows the injustice of imputing to me the assassinations that were committed, because, it is said, as chief, I could have prevented them; but am I responsible for the evil that was done in my absence and without my knowledge?

While at Gonaïves (at the commencement of hostilities), I sent my aide-de-camp, Couppé, to Gen. Dessalines, to bid him order the commander of Léogane to take all the inhabitants, men and women, and send them to Port Républicain; to muster all the armed men he could in that place, and prepare himself for a most vigorous resistance in case of attack. My aide-de-camp, Couppé, bearer of my orders, returned and told me that he had not found Gen. Dessalines, but had learned that Léogane had been burned, and that the inhabitants had escaped to Port Républicain.

All these disasters happened just at the time that Gen. Leclerc came. Why did he not inform me of his powers before landing? Why did he land without my order and in defiance of the order of the Commission? Did he not commit the first hostilities? Did he not seek to gain over the generals and other officers under my command by every possible means? Did he not try to instigate the labourers to rise, by persuading them that I treated them like slaves, and that he had come to break their chains? Ought he to have employed such means in a country where peace and tranquillity reigned? – in a country which was in the power of the Republic?

If I did oblige my fellow countrymen to work, it was to teach them the value of true liberty without license; it was to prevent corruption of morals; it was for the general happiness of the island, for the interest of the Republic. And I had effectually succeeded in my undertaking, since there could not be found in all the colony a single man unemployed, and the number of beggars had diminished to such a degree that, apart from a few in the towns, not a single one was to be found in the country.

If Gen. Leclerc's intentions had been good, would he have received Golart into his army, and given to him the command of the Ninth demi-brigade, a corps that he had raised at the time that he was chief of battalion? Would he have employed this dangerous rebel, who caused proprietors to be assassinated in their own dwelling places; who invaded the town of Môle-Saint-Nicolas; who fired upon Gen. Clerveaux, who commanded there; upon Gen. Maurepas and his brigade commander; who made war upon the labourers of Jean-Rabel, from Moustiques and the heights of Port-de-Paix; who carried his audacity so far as to oppose me when I marched against him to force him to submit to his chief, and to retake the territory and the town which he had invaded! The day that he dared to fire upon me, a ball cut the plume from my hat; Bondère, a physician, who accompanied me, was killed at my side, my aides-de-camp were unhorsed. In short, this brigand, after being steeped in every crime, concealed himself in a forest; he only came out of it upon the arrival of the French squadron. Ought Gen. Leclerc to have raised likewise to the rank of brigade commander another rebel, called L'Amour Desrances, who had caused all the inhabitants of the Plain of Cul-de-Sac to be assassinated; who urged the labourers to revolt; who pillaged all this part of the island; against whom, only two months before the arrival of the squadron, I had been obliged to march, and whom I forced to hide in the forests? Why were rebels and others amicably received, while my subordinates and myself, who remained steadfastly faithful to the French government, and who had maintained order and tranquillity, were attacked? Why was it made a crime to have executed the orders of the government? Why was all the evil that had been done and the disorders that had existed imputed to me? All these facts are known by every inhabitant of St-Domingue. Why, on arriving, did they not go to the root of the evil? Had the troops that gave themselves up to Gen. Leclerc received the order from me? Did they consult me? No. Well! those who committed the wrong did not consult me. It is not right to attribute to me more wrong than I deserve.

I shared these reflections with some prisoners I had. They replied that it was my influence upon the people that was feared, and that these violent means were employed to destroy it. This caused me new reflections. Considering all the misfortunes the colony had already suffered, the dwellings destroyed, assassinations committed, the violence exercised even upon women, I forgot all the wrongs that had been done me, to think only of the happiness of the island and the interest of the government. I determined to obey the order of the First Consul, since Gen. Leclerc had just withdrawn from the Cap with all his forces, after the affair of Crête-à-Pierrot.

Let it be observed that up to this time I had not been able to find an instant in which to reply to the First Consul. I seized with eagerness this momentary quiet to do so. I assured the First Consul of my submission and entire devotion to his orders, but represented to him 'that if he did not send another older general to take command, the resistance which I must continue to oppose to Gen. Leclerc would tend to increase the prevalent disorder'.

I remembered then that Gen. Dessalines had reported to me that two officers of the squadron – one an aide-de-camp of Gen. Boudet, the other a naval officer, accompanied by two dragoons, sent to stir up a rebellion among the troops – had been made prisoners at the time of the evacuation of Port-au-Prince. I ordered them to be brought before me, and, after conversing with them, sent them back to Gen. Boudet, sending by them a letter with the one that I had written to the First Consul. Just as I was sending off these two officers, I learned that Gen. Hardy had passed Coupe-à-l'Inde with his army, that he had attacked my possessions, devastated them, and taken away all my animals, among them a horse named Bel-Argent, which I valued very highly. Without losing time, I marched against him with the force I had. I overtook him near Dondon. A fierce engagement took place, which lasted from eleven in the morning till six in the evening.

Before setting out, I had ordered Gen. Dessalines to join the troops who had evacuated Crête-à-Pierrot, and go into camp at Camp-Marchand, informing him that after the battle I should proceed to Marmelade.

Upon my arrival in that place, I received the reply of Gen. Boudet, which he sent me by my nephew Chancy, whom he had previously made a prisoner.

That general assured me that my letter would easily reach the First Consul, that, to effect this, he had already sent it to Gen. Leclerc, who had promised him to forward it. Upon the report of my nephew, and after reading the letter of Gen. Boudet, I thought I recognized in him a character of honesty and frankness worthy of a French officer qualified to command. Therefore I addressed myself to him with confidence, begging him to persuade Gen. Leclerc to enter upon terms of conciliation with me. I assured him that ambition had never been my guide, but only honour; that I was ready to give up the command in obedience to the orders of the First Consul, and to make all necessary sacrifices to arrest the progress of the evil. I sent him this letter by my nephew Chancy, whom he kept with him. Two days later, I received a letter sent in haste by an orderly, announcing to me that he had made known my intentions to Gen. Leclerc, and assuring me that the latter was ready to make terms with me, and that I could depend upon the good intentions of the government with regard to me.

The same day, Gen. Christophe communicated to me a letter he had just received from a citizen named Vilton, living at Petite-Anse, and another from Gen. Hardy, both asking him for an interview. I gave permission to Gen. Christophe to hold these interviews, recommending him to be very circumspect.

Gen. Christophe did not meet this appointment with Gen. Hardy, for he received a letter from Gen. Leclerc, proposing to him another rendezvous. He sent me a copy of this letter and of his reply, and asked my permission to report himself at the place indicated; which I granted, and he went.

Gen. Christophe, on his return, brought me a letter from Gen. Leclerc, saying that he should feel highly satisfied if he could induce me to concert with him, and submit to the orders of the Republic. I replied immediately that I had always been submissive to the French government, as I had invariably borne arms for it;[3] that if from the beginning I had been treated as I should have been, not a single shot would have been fired; that peace would not have been even disturbed in the island, and that the intention of the government would have been fulfilled. In short, I showed to Gen. Leclerc, as well as to Gen. Christophe, all my indignation at the course the latter had pursued, without orders from me.

The next day, I sent to Gen. Leclerc my adjutant-general Fontaine, bearer of a second letter, in which I asked for an interview at Héricourt, which he refused. Fontaine assured me, however, that he had been well received. I was not discouraged. I sent the third time my aide-de-camp Couppé and my secretary Nathand, assuring him that I was ready to give up the command to him, conformably to the intentions of the First Consul. He replied that an hour of conversation would be worth more than ten letters, giving me his word of honour that he would act with all the frankness and loyalty that could be expected of a French general. At the same time a proclamation from him was brought me, bidding all citizens to regard as null and void that article of the proclamation of 16 February 1802 that made me an outlaw. 'Do not fear,' he said in this proclamation, 'you and your generals, and the people who are with you, that I shall search out the past conduct of anyone; I will draw the veil of oblivion over the events that have taken place at St-Domingue; I imitate, in so doing, the example the First Consul gave to France on 11 November. In the future, I wish to see in the island only good citizens. You ask for repose; after having borne the burden of government so long, repose is due you; but I hope that in your retirement you will use your wisdom, in your moments of leisure, for the prosperity of St-Domingue.'

After this proclamation and the word of honour of the general, I proceeded to the Cap. I submitted myself to Gen. Leclerc in accordance with the wish of the First Consul; I afterward talked with him with all the frankness and cordiality of a soldier who loves and esteems his comrade. He promised me forgetfulness of the past and the protection of the French government. He agreed with me that we had both been wrong. 'You can, General,' he said to me, 'retire to your home in perfect security. But tell me if Gen. Dessalines will obey my orders, and if I can rely upon him?' I replied that he could; that Gen. Dessalines might have faults, like every man, but that he understood military subordination. I suggested to him, however, that for the public good and to re-establish the labourers in their occupations, as they were at the time of his arrival in the island, it was necessary that Gen. Dessalines should be recalled to his command at St-Marc, and Gen. Charles Belair to L'Arcahaye, which he promised me should be done. At eleven in the evening, I took leave of him and withdrew to Héricourt, where I passed the night with Gen. Fressinet, and set out the next morning for Marmelade.

The third day after, I received a letter from Gen. Leclerc, bidding me discharge my foot-guards and horse-guards. He addressed to me also an order for Gen. Dessalines; I acquainted myself with it and sent it to Gen. Dessalines, telling him to comply with it. And that I might the better fulfil the promises that I had made Gen. Leclerc, I requested Gen. Dessalines to meet me halfway between his house and mine. I urged him to submit, as I had done; I told him that the public interest required me to make great sacrifices, and that I was willing to make them; but as for him, he might keep his command. I said as much to Gen. Charles, also to all the officers with them; finally, I persuaded them, in spite of all the reluctance and regret they evinced, to leave me and go away. They even shed tears. After this interview, all returned to their own homes. Adjutant-General Perrin, whom Gen. Leclerc had sent to Dessalines with his orders, found him very ready to comply with them, since I had previously engaged him to do so in our interview. As we have seen, a promise was made to place Gen. Charles at L'Arcahaye; however, it was not fulfilled.

It was unnecessary for me to order the inhabitants of Dondon, St-Michel, St-Raphaël and Marmelade to return to their homes, since they had done so as soon as I had taken possession of these communities; I only advised them to resume their usual occupations. I ordered also the inhabitants of Plaisance, and the neighbouring places, to return home and begin their labour too. They expressed fears that they might be disturbed. Therefore I wrote to Gen. Leclerc, reminding him of his promise and begging him to attend to their execution. He replied that his orders were already given upon that subject. Meanwhile, the commander of this place had divided his forces and sent detachments into all the districts, which had alarmed the labourers and compelled them to flee to the mountains. I proceeded to Ennery and acquainted Gen. Leclerc with these things, as I had promised him. In this town I found a great many labourers from Gonaïves, whom I persuaded to return home. Before I left Marmelade, I ordered the commander of that place to restore the artillery and ammunition to the commander of Plaisance, in conformity to the desire of Gen. Leclerc. I also ordered the commander at Ennery to return the only piece of artillery there, and also the ammunition, to the commander of Gonaïves.

I then employed myself in rebuilding my houses which had been burned. In a house in the mountains, which had escaped the flames, I had to prepare a comfortable lodging for my wife, who was still in the woods where she had been obliged to take refuge.

While engaged in these occupations, I learned that five hundred troops had arrived, to be stationed at Ennery, a little town, which, until then, could not have had more than fifty armed men as a police force; and that a very large detachment had also been sent to St-Michel. I hastened to the town. I saw that all my houses had been pillaged and even the coffers of my labourers carried off. At the very moment when I was entering my complaint to the commander, I pointed out to him the soldiers loaded with fruit of all kinds, even unripe fruit; I also showed him the labourers who, seeing these robberies, were fleeing to other houses in the mountains. I gave an account to Gen. Leclerc of what was going on, and observed to him that the measures that were being taken, far from inspiring confidence, only increased distrust; that the number of troops he had sent was very considerable, and could only be an injury to agriculture and the inhabitants. I then returned to my house in the mountains.

The next day I received, in this house, a visit from the commander at Ennery, and I saw very clearly that this soldier, instead of making me a courtesy visit, had come to my house merely to reconnoitre my dwelling and the avenues about it, that he might seize me the more easily when he received the order to do so. While talking with him, I was informed that several soldiers had gone with horses and other beasts of burden to one of my residences near the town, where a god-daughter of mine was residing, and had taken away the coffee and other provisions found there. I complained to him; he promised me to put a stop to these robberies and to punish severely those who had been guilty of them. Fearing that my house in the mountains inspired only distrust, I determined to remove to that very house that had just been pillaged, and almost totally destroyed, but two hundred paces from the town. I left my wife in the house which I had prepared for her. I was now occupied in laying out new plantations to replace those that had been destroyed, and in preparing necessary materials for reconstructing my buildings. But every day I experienced new robberies and new vexations. The soldiers came to my house in such large numbers that I dared not have them arrested. In vain I bore my complaints to the commander. I received no satisfaction. Finally, I determined, though Gen. Leclerc had not done me the honour of answering my two earlier letters upon this subject, to write him a third, which I sent to him at the Cap by my son Placide, for greater security. This, like the others, elicited no reply. But the chief of staff told me that he would make his report. Some time after, the commander, having come to see me again one afternoon, found me at the head of my labourers, employed in directing the work of reconstruction. He himself saw my son Isaac drive away several soldiers who had just come to the gate to cut down the bananas and figs. I repeated to him the most earnest complaints. He still promised to stop these disorders. During the three weeks that I stayed in this place, I witnessed daily new ravages; every day I received visits from people who came as spies, but they were all witnesses that I was engaged solely in domestic labours. Gen. Brunet himself came, and found me occupied in the same manner. Notwithstanding my conduct, I received a letter from Gen. Leclerc which, in place of giving me satisfaction in regard to the complaints I had made to him, accused me of keeping armed men within the borders of Ennery, and ordered me to send them away. Persuaded of my innocence, and that evil-disposed people had deceived him, I replied that I had too much honour to break promises I had made, and that when I gave up the command to him, it was not without reflection; that, moreover, I had no intention of trying to take it back. I assured him, besides, that I had no knowledge of armed men in the environs of Ennery, and that for three weeks I had been constantly at work on my own place. I sent my son Isaac to give him an account of all the vexations I suffered, and to warn him that if he did not put an end to them, I should be obliged to leave the place where I was living, and go to my ranch in the Spanish part.

One day, before I received any answer from Gen. Leclerc, I was informed that one of his aides-de-camp, passing by Ennery, had told the commander that he was the bearer of an order for my arrest, addressed to Gen. Brunet. Gen. Leclerc having given his word of honour and promised the protection of the French government, I refused to believe the report; I even said to someone who advised me to leave my residence, that I had promised to stay there quietly, working to repair the havoc that had been made; that I had not given up the command and sent away my troops to act so foolishly now; that I did not wish to leave home, and if they came to arrest me, they would find me there; that, besides, I would not give credence to the calumny.

The next day I received a second letter from Gen. Leclerc, by my son whom I sent to him, which read thus:

Army Of St-Domingue

Headquarters At Cap Français, 5 June 1802
The Gen.-in-Chief to Gen. Toussaint:
Since you persist, Citizen-General, in thinking that the great number of troops stationed at Plaisance (the secretary probably wrote Plaisance by mistake, meaning Ennery) frightens the labourers of that district, I have commissioned Gen. Brunet to act in concert with you, and to place a part of these troops in the rear of Gonaïves and one detachment at Plaisance. Let the labourers understand, that, having taken this measure, I shall punish those who leave their dwellings to go to the mountains. Let me know, as soon as this order has been executed, the results which it produces, because, if the means of persuasion that you employ do not succeed, I shall use military measures. I salute you.

The same day I received a letter from Gen. Brunet, of which the following is an extract:

Army of St-Domingue,

Headquarters at Georges, 7 June 1802
Brunet, Gen. Of Division, to the Gen. Of Division,
Toussaint L'Ouverture
Now is the time, Citizen-General, to make known unquestionably to the General-in-Chief that those who wish to

deceive him in regard to your fidelity are base calumniators, and that your sentiments tend to restore order and tranquillity in your neighbourhood. You must assist me in securing free communication to the Cap, which has been interrupted since yesterday, three persons having been murdered by fifty brigands between Ennery and Coupe-à-Pintade. Send in pursuit of these murderers men worthy of confidence, whom you are to pay well; I will keep account of your expenses.

We have arrangements to make together, my dear General, which it is impossible to do by letter, but which an hour's conference would complete. If I were not worn out by labour and petty cares, I should have been the bearer of my own letter today; but not being able to leave at this time, will you not come to me? If you have recovered from your indisposition, let it be tomorrow; when a good work is to be done, there should be no delay. You will not find in my country house all the comforts I could desire before receiving you, but you will find the sincerity of an honest man who desires only the prosperity of the colony and your own happiness. If Madame Toussaint, whom I greatly desire to know, wishes to make the journey, it will give me pleasure. If she needs horses, I will send her mine. I repeat, General, you will never find a sincerer friend than myself.

With confidence in the Captain-General, with friendship for all who are under him, and hoping that you may enjoy peace,

I cordially salute you.

Brunet

P. S. Your servant who has gone to Port-au-Prince passed here this morning; he left with his passport made out in due form.

That very servant, instead of receiving his passport, was arrested, and is now in prison with me.

After reading these two letters, although not very well, I yielded to the solicitations of my sons and others, and set out the same night to see Gen. Brunet, accompanied by two officers only. At eight in the evening I arrived at the general's house. When he met me, I told him that I had received his letter, and also that of the General-in-Chief, requesting me to act with him, and that I had come for that purpose; that I had not brought my wife, as he requested, because she never left home, being much occupied with domestic duties, but if sometime, when he was travelling, he would do her the honour of visiting her, she would receive him with pleasure. I said to him that, being ill, my stay must be short, asking him, therefore, to finish our business as soon as possible, that I might return.

I handed him the letter of Gen. Leclerc. After reading it, he told me that he had not yet received any order to act in concert with me upon the subject of the letter; he then excused himself for a moment, and went out, after calling an officer to keep me company. He had hardly left the room when an aide-de-camp of Gen. Leclerc entered, accompanied by a large number of soldiers, who surrounded me, seized me, bound me as a criminal, and conducted me on board the frigate *Créole*.

I claimed the protection that Gen. Brunet, on his word of honour, had promised me, but without avail. I saw him no more. He had probably concealed himself to escape my well-merited reproaches. I afterwards learned that he treated my family with great cruelty; that, immediately after my arrest, he sent a detachment of troops to the house where I had been living with a part of my family, mostly women, children and labourers, and ordered them to set it on fire, compelling the unhappy victims to fly half-naked to the woods; that everything had been pillaged and sacked; that the aide-de-camp of Gen. Brunet had even taken from my house fifty-five ounces of gold belonging to me, and thirty-three ounces belonging to one of my nieces, together with all the linen of the family.

Having committed these outrages upon my dwelling, the commander at Ennery went, at the head of one hundred men, to the house occupied by my wife and nieces, and arrested them, without giving them time to collect any of their effects. They were conducted like criminals to Gonaïves and put on board the frigate *Guerrière*.

When I was arrested, I had no extra clothing with me. I wrote to my wife, asking her to send me such things as I should need most to Cap Français, hoping I should be taken there. This note I sent by an aide-de-camp of Gen. Leclerc, begging that it might be allowed to pass; it did not reach its destination, and I received nothing.

As soon as I was taken on board the *Créole*, we set sail, and, four leagues from the Cap, found the *Héros*, to which they transferred me. The next day, my wife and my children, who had been arrested with her, arrived there also. We immediately set sail for France. After a voyage of thirty-two days – during which I endured not only great fatigue, but also every species of hardship, while my wife and children received treatment from which their sex and rank should have preserved them – instead of allowing us to land, they retained us on board sixty-seven days.

After such treatment, could I not justly ask where were the promises of Gen. Leclerc? Where was the protection of the French government? If they no longer needed my services and wished to replace me, should they not have treated me as white French generals are always treated? They are warned when they are to be relieved of their command; a messenger is sent to notify them to resign the command to such-and-such persons; and in case they refuse to obey, measures are taken to compel them; they can then justly be treated as rebels and sent to France.

I have, in fact, known some generals guilty of criminally neglecting their duties, but who, in consideration of their character, have escaped punishment until they could be brought before superior authority.

Should not Gen. Leclerc have informed me that various charges had been brought against me? Should he not have said to me, 'I gave you my word of honour and promised you the protection of the government; today, as you have been found guilty, I am going to send you to that government to give an account of your conduct'? Or, 'The government orders you to submit; I convey that order to you'?[4] I have not been so treated; on the other hand, means have been employed against me that are only used against the greatest criminals. Doubtless, I owe this treatment to my colour; but my colour, my colour, has it hindered me from serving my country with zeal and fidelity? Does the colour of my skin impair my honour and my bravery?

But even supposing that I was a criminal, and that the government had ordered my arrest, was it necessary to employ a hundred riflemen to arrest my wife and children in their own home, without regard to their sex, age and rank; without humanity and without charity? Was it necessary to burn my houses, and to pillage and sack my possessions? No. My wife, my children, my family had no responsibility in the matter; they were not accountable to the government; it was not lawful to arrest them.

Gen. Leclerc's authority was undisputed; did he fear me as a rival? I can but compare him to the Roman Senate, pursuing Hannibal to the very depths of his retreat.

Upon the arrival of the squadron in the colony, they took advantage of my absence to seize a part of my correspondence, which was at Port Républicain; another portion, which was in one of my houses, has also been seized since my arrest. Why have they not sent me with this correspondence to give an account of my movements? They have taken forcible possession of my papers in order to charge me with crimes which I have never committed; but I have nothing to fear; this correspondence is sufficient to justify me. They have sent me to France destitute of everything; they have seized my property and my papers, and have spread atrocious calumnies concerning me. Is it not like cutting off a man's legs and telling him to walk? Is it not like cutting out a man's tongue and telling him to talk? Is it not burying a man alive?

In regard to the constitution, the subject of one charge against me: Having driven from the colony the enemies of the Republic, calmed the factions and united all parties; perceiving, after I had taken possession of St-Domingue, that the government made no laws for the colony, and feeling the necessity of police regulations for the security and tranquillity of the people, I called an assembly of wise and learned men, composed of deputies from all the communities, to conduct this business. When this assembly met, I represented to its members that they had an arduous and responsible task before them; that they were to make laws adapted to the country, advantageous to the government, and beneficial to all – laws suited to the localities, to the character and customs of the inhabitants. The constitution must be submitted for the sanction of the government, which alone had the right to adopt or reject it. Therefore, as soon as the constitution was decided upon and its laws fixed, I sent the whole, by a member of the assembly, to the government, to obtain its sanction. The errors or faults which this constitution may contain cannot therefore be imputed to me. At the time of Leclerc's arrival, I had heard nothing from the government upon this subject. Why today do they seek to make a crime of that which is no crime? Why put truth for falsehood, and falsehood for truth? Why put darkness for light and light for darkness?

In a conversation which I had at the Cap with Gen. Leclerc, he told me that while at Samana he had sent a spy to Santo

Domingo to learn if I was there, who brought back word that I was. Why did he not go there to find me and give me the orders of the First Consul, before commencing hostilities? He knew my readiness to obey orders. Instead of this, he took advantage of my absence from St-Domingue to proceed to the Cap and send troops to all parts of the colony. This conduct proves that he had no intention of communicating anything to me.

If Gen. Leclerc went to the colony to do evil, it should not be charged upon me. It is true that only one of us can be blamed; but however little one may wish to do me justice, it is clear that he is the author of all the evils the island has suffered since, without warning me, he entered the colony, which he found in a state of prosperity, fell upon the inhabitants, who were at their work, contributing to the welfare of the community, and shed their blood upon their native soil. That is the true source of the evil.

If two children were quarrelling together, should not their father or mother stop them, find out which was the aggressor, and punish him, or punish them, if they were both wrong? Gen. Leclerc had no right to arrest me; the government alone could arrest us both, hear us and judge us. Yet Gen. Leclerc enjoys liberty, and I am in a dungeon.

Having given an account of my conduct since the arrival of the fleet at St-Domingue, I will enter into some details of previous events.

Since I entered the service of the Republic, I have not claimed a penny of my salary; Gen. Laveaux, government agents, all responsible persons connected with the public treasury, can do me this justice, that no one has been more prudent, more disinterested than I. I have only now and then received the extra pay allowed me; very often I have not asked even this. Whenever I have taken money from the treasury, it has been for some public use; the governor of finances [*l'ordonnateur*] has used it as the service required. I remember that once only, when far from home, I borrowed six thousand francs from Citizen Smith, who was governor of the Department of the South.

I will sum up, in a few words, my conduct and the results of my administration. At the time of the evacuation of the English, there was not a penny in the public treasury; money had to be borrowed to pay the troops and the officers of the Republic. When Gen. Leclerc arrived, he found three million, five hundred thousand francs in the public funds. When I returned to Cayes, after the departure of Gen. Rigaud, the treasury was empty; Gen. Leclerc found three millions there; he found proportionate sums in all the private depositories on the island. Thus it is seen that I did not serve my country from interested motives; but, on the contrary, I served it with honour, fidelity and integrity, sustained by the hope of receiving, at some future day, flattering acknowledgments from the government; all who know me will do me this justice.

I have been a slave; I am willing to own it; but I have never received reproaches from my masters.

I have neglected nothing at St-Domingue for the welfare of the island; I have robbed myself of rest to contribute to it; I have sacrificed everything for it. I have made it my duty and pleasure to develop the resources of this beautiful colony. Zeal, activity, courage – I have employed them all.

The island was invaded by the enemies of the Republic; I had then but a thousand men, armed with pikes. I sent them back to labour in the field, and organized several regiments, by the authority of Gen. Laveaux.

The Spanish portion had joined the English to make war upon the French. Gen. Desfourneaux was sent to attack St-Michel with well-disciplined troops of the line; he could not take it. General Laveaux ordered me to the attack; I carried it. It is to be remarked that, at the time of the attack by Gen. Desfourneaux, the place was not fortified, and that when I took it, it was fortified by bastions in every corner. I also took St-Raphaël and

Hinche, and rendered an account to Gen. Laveaux. The English were entrenched at Pont-de-l'Ester; I drove them from the place. They were in possession of Petite Rivière. My ammunition consisted of one case of cartridges which had fallen into the water on my way to the attack; this did not discourage me. I carried the place by assault before day, with my dragoons, and made all the garrison prisoners. I sent them to Gen. Laveaux. I had but one piece of cannon; I took nine at Petite Rivière. Among the posts gained at Petite Rivière, was a fortification defended by seven pieces of cannon, which I attacked, and carried by assault. I also conquered the Spaniards entrenched in the camps of Miraut and Dubourg at Verrettes. I won an important victory over the English in a battle that lasted from six in the morning until nearly night. This battle was so fierce that the roads were filled with the dead, and rivers of blood were seen on every side. I took all the baggage and ammunition of the enemy, and a large number of prisoners. I sent the whole to Gen. Laveaux, giving him an account of the engagement. All the posts of the English upon the heights of St-Marc were taken by me; the walled fortifications in the mountains of Fond-Baptiste and Délices, the camp of Drouët in the Matheux mountains, which the English regarded as impregnable, the citadels of Mirebalais, called the Gibraltar of the island, occupied by eleven hundred men, the celebrated camp of l'Acul-du-Saut, the stone fortifications of Trou-d'Eau, three storeys high, those of the camp of Décayette and of Beau-Bien – in short, all the fortifications of the English in this quarter were unable to withstand me, as were those of Neybe, of Saint Jean de la Maguâna, of Las Mathas, of Banique and other places occupied by the Spaniards; all were brought by me under the power of the Republic. I was also exposed to the greatest dangers; several times I narrowly escaped being made prisoner; I shed my blood for my country; I received a ball in the right hip which remains there still; I received a violent blow on the head from a cannonball, which knocked out the greater part of my teeth, and loosened the rest. In short, I received upon different occasions seventeen wounds, whose honourable scars still remain. Gen. Laveaux witnessed many of my engagements; he is too honourable not to do me justice: ask him if I ever hesitated to endanger my life, when the good of my country and the triumph of the Republic required it.

If I were to record the various services which I have rendered the government, I should need many volumes, and even then should not finish them; and, as a reward for all these services, I have been arbitrarily arrested in St-Domingue, bound, and put on board ship like a criminal, without regard for my rank, without the least consideration. Is this the recompense due my labours? Should my conduct lead me to expect such treatment?

I was once rich. At the time of the revolution, I was worth six hundred and forty-eight thousand francs. I spent it in the service of my country. I purchased but one small estate upon which to establish my wife and family. Today, notwithstanding my disinterestedness, they seek to cover me with opprobrium and infamy; I am made the most unhappy of men; my liberty is taken from me; I am separated from all that I hold dearest in the world – from a venerable father, 105 years old, who needs my assistance, from a dearly loved wife who, I fear, separated from me cannot endure the afflictions that overwhelm her, and from a cherished family, who made the happiness of my life.

On my arrival in France I wrote to the First Consul and to the Minister of the Navy, giving them an account of my situation, and asking their assistance for my family and myself. Undoubtedly, they felt the justice of my request, and gave orders that what I asked should be furnished me. But, instead of this, I have received the old half-worn dress of a soldier, and shoes in the same condition. Did I need this humiliation added to my misfortune?

When I left the ship, I was put into a carriage. I hoped then that I was to be taken before a tribunal to give an account of my conduct, and to be judged. Far from it; without a moment's rest I was taken to a fort on the frontiers of the Republic, and confined in a frightful dungeon.

It is from the depths of this dreary prison that I appeal to the justice and magnanimity of the First Consul. He is too noble and too good a general to turn away from an old soldier, covered with wounds in the service of his country, without giving him the opportunity to justify himself, and to have judgement pronounced upon him.

I ask, then, to be brought before a tribunal or council of war, before which, also, Gen. Leclerc may appear, and that we may both be judged after we have both been heard; equity, reason, law all assure me that this justice cannot be refused me.

In passing through France, I have seen in the newspapers an article concerning myself. I am accused in this article of being a rebel and a traitor, and, to justify the accusation, a letter is said to have been intercepted in which I encouraged the labourers of St-Domingue to revolt. I never wrote such a letter, and I defy anyone to produce it, to tell me to whom it was addressed, and to bring forward the person. As to the rest of the calumny, it falls of itself; if I had intended to make war, would I have laid down my arms and submitted? No reasonable man, much less a soldier, can believe such an absurdity.

ADDITION TO THE MEMOIRS

If the government had sent a wiser man, there would have been no trouble; not a single shot would have been fired.

Why did fear occasion so much injustice on the part of Gen. Leclerc? Why did he violate his word of honour? Upon the arrival of the frigate *Guerrière*, which brought my wife, why did I see on board a number of people who had been arrested with her? Many of these persons had not fired a shot. They were innocent men, fathers of families, who had been torn from the arms of their wives and children. All these persons had shed their blood to preserve the colony to France; they were officers of my staff, my secretaries, who had done nothing but by my orders; all, therefore, were arrested without cause.

Upon landing at Brest, my wife and children were sent to different destinations, of both of which I am ignorant. The government should do me more justice: my wife and children have done nothing and have nothing to answer for; they should be sent home to watch over our interests. Gen. Leclerc has occasioned all this evil; but I am at the bottom of a dungeon, unable to justify myself. The government is too just to keep my hands tied, and allow Gen. Leclerc to abuse me thus, without listening to me.

Everybody has told me that this government was just; should I not, then, share its justice and its benefits?

Gen. Leclerc has said in the letter to the minister, which I have seen in the newspaper, that I was waiting for his troops to grow sick, in order to make war and take back the command. This is an atrocious and abominable lie: it is a cowardly act on his part. Although I may not have much knowledge or much education, I have enough good sense to hinder me from contending against the will of my government; I never thought of it. The French government is too strong, too powerful, for Gen. Leclerc to think me opposed to it, who am its servant. It is true that when Gen. Leclerc marched against me, I said several times that I should make no attack, that I should only defend myself, until July or August; that then I would commence in my turn. But, afterwards, I reflected upon the misfortunes of the colony and upon the letter of the First Consul; I then submitted.

I repeat it again: I demand that Gen. Leclerc and myself be judged before a tribunal; that the government should order all my correspondence to be brought; by this means my innocence, and all that I have done for the Republic will be seen, although I know that several letters have been intercepted.

First Consul, father of all soldiers, upright judge, defender of innocence, pronounce my destiny. My wounds are deep; apply to them the healing remedy which will prevent them from opening anew; you are the physician; I rely entirely upon your justice and wisdom!

NOTES

INTRODUCTION

1. Marika Sherwood and Hakim Adi, *Pan-African History: Political Figures from Africa and the Diaspora since 1787* (Routledge, 2003), p. 109.
2. Arthur L. Stinchcombe, *Sugar Island Slavery in the Age of Enlightenment: The Political Economy of the Caribbean World* (Princeton University Press, 1995), p. 201.
3. See publications by James Bugental: *The Search for Authenticity* (Hold, Rinehart & Winston, 1965); *The Search for Existential Identity* (Jossey-Bass, Inc., 1976); *Psychotherapy and Process* (Longman Higher Education, 1978); *The Art of the Psychotherapist* (W.W. Norton & Co. Ltd, 1987); *Psychotherapy Isn't What You Think* (Zeig, Tucker & Co., 1999).
4. Stinchcombe, *Sugar Island Slavery*, p. 231.
5. Laurent Dubois, *Avengers of the New World* (Belknap Press of Harvard University/Duke University, 2004), p. 3, citing Aimé Césaire, *Toussaint Louverture: La révolution française et le problème colonial* (Le club français du livre, 1960).
6. Dubois, *Avengers of the New World*, p. 176.
7. Chris Bongie, *Islands and Exiles: The Creole Identities of Post/Colonial Literature* (Stanford University Press, 1998, p. 3).
8. Stinchcombe, *Sugar Island Slavery*, p. 319.
9. Franklin W. Knight and Colin A. Palmer, eds, *The Modern Caribbean* (University of North Carolina Press, 1989), p. 21.
10. Ron Eyerman, *Cultural Trauma: Slavery and the Formation of African American Identity* (Cambridge University Press, 2001), p. 1.

11. Frantz Fanon, *Black Skin, White Masks*, transl. Charles Lam Markmann (Grove Press, 1967; originally published in 1952).
12. Ben Shalit, *The Psychology of Conflict and Combat* (Praeger, 1988), p. 8.
13. C. L. R. James, *The Black Jacobins* (Allison & Busby, 1982), pp. 211–13.
14. Joanne B. Ciulla, ed., *Ethics: The Heart of Leadership* (Praeger, 1998), p. 87.
15. Dubois, *Avengers of the New World*, p. 217.
16. Richard Jenkins, *Social Identity* (Routledge, 2004), p. 27.
17. Karl E. Scheibe, *The Psychology of Self and Identity* (Praeger, 1995), p. 23.
18. William Easterly, *The White Man's Burden* (Penguin, 2006).
19. A Kiswahili word meaning 'coloured people'.
20. Scheibe, *Psychology of Self and Identity*, p. 113.
21. Kenneth R. Hoover, James Marcia and Kristen Parris, *The Power of Identity: Politics in a New Key* (Chatham House Publishers, 1997), p. 13.
22. Ibid, p. 61.
23. A Zulu word meaning 'humanity'; a shared principle of humanity.
24. President Thabo Mbeki, in *ANC Today*, vol. 7, no. 14 (13–19 April 2007).
25. Molefi Kete Asante, *The Haitian Revolution and President Jean-Bertrand Aristide* (City Press, 2004).
26. Randall Robinson, *An Unbroken Agony* (Basic Civitas Books, 2007), p. 7.
27. Dominic Abrams, Michael A. Hogg and Jose M. Marques, eds, *The Social Psychology of Inclusion and Exclusion* (Psychology Press, 2005), p. 27.
28. J. N. Pieterse, *Globalization or Empire?* (Routledge, 2004), p. 61.
29. H. J. Sindima, *Religious and Political Ethics in Africa: A Moral Inquiry* (Greenwood Press, 1998), p. 1.
30. Ibid., p. 69.
31. See Madison Smartt Bell, *Toussaint Louverture: A Biography* (Pantheon, 2007).
32. A. Kenny, *Reasons and Religion: Essays in Philosophical Theology* (Blackwell, 1987), p. 37.
33. H. Schear, ed., *Religion and the Cure of Souls in Jung's Psychology* (Pantheon Books, 1950), p. 137.
34. Ibid., p. 970.

35. G. Vernon, *Sociology of Religion* (McGraw-Hill, 1962), p. 77.
36. Peter C. Hodgson, *Hegel and Christian Theology: A Reading of the Lectures on the Philosophy of Religion* (Oxford University Press, 2005), p. 5.
37. R. Homan, *The Sociology of Religion: A Bibliographical Survey* (Greenwood Press, 1986), p. 3.
38. R. Hall, *The Love of Philosophy and the Philosophy of Love: Kierkegaard, Cavell, Nussbaum* (Pennsylvania State University Press, 2000), p. 9.
39. G. Gutiérrez, *We Drink from Our Own Wells: The Spiritual Journey of a People*, transl. M. J. O'Connell (Orbis Books, 1984), p. 72.
40. Massimo Livi-Bacci and Gustavo De Santis, eds, *Population and Poverty in the Developing World* (Clarendon Press, 1998), p. 25.
41. Mark Robert Rank, *One Nation, Underprivileged: Why American Poverty Affects Us All* (Oxford University Press, 2004), p. 49.
42. Adam Smith, *An Inquiry into the Nature and Causes of the Wealth of Nations*, ed. C. J. Bullock (P. F. Collier & Son, 1909), p. 414.
43. Maurice Parmelee, *Poverty and Social Progress* (Macmillan, 1916), p. 7.
44. Ibid., p. 48.
45. Richard P. Bentall, Loren R. Mosher and John Read, eds, *Models of Madness: Psychological, Social and Biological Approaches to Schizophrenia* (Brunner-Routledge, 2004), p. 161.
46. E. Wayne Nafziger and Raimo Väyrynen, eds, *The Prevention of Humanitarian Emergencies* (Palgrave, 2002), p. 43.
47. Tom Ricker, 'The IDB and Haiti: Deliver us from Debt', 11 June 2007 (HaitiAnalysis.com).
48. Ibid.
49. Zulu.

NOTE ON THE TEXTS

1. As I write this, the most informed and balanced overview of the current state of knowledge about Toussaint L'Ouverture is David Geggus's short piece, 'Toussaint L'Ouverture and the Haitian Revolution', in R. William Weisberger, ed., *Profiles of Revolutionaries in Atlantic History, 1750–1850* (Columbia University Press, 2007), pp. 115–35.
2. Deborah Jenson, 'Toussaint Louverture, Spin Doctor? Launching

the Haitian Revolution in the French Media', in Doris Garraway, ed., *Tree of Liberty: Legacies of the Haitian Revolution in the Atlantic World* (University of Virginia Press, 2008), pp. 41–62.

3. Ibid., p. 49.

4. Madison Smartt Bell, *Toussaint Louverture: A Biography* (Pantheon Books, 2007), p. 197.

5. 21 August 1789, *Lettres du Comte de Mirabeau à ses commetans*. Personal correspondence with the editor, Marcel Dorigny, 30 November 2007

6. François Furet, *Penser la Révolution française* (Gallimard, 1978).

7. I develop this analysis of the Haitian Revolution further in *Universal Emancipation: The Haitian Revolution and the Radical Enlightenment* (University of Virginia Press, 2008).

I PROCLAMATION, 29 AUGUST 1793

1. Vincent Ogé (*c*. 1750–91), Haitian revolutionist and national hero. A free mulatto, well educated and comparatively wealthy, he was sent to plead before the National Assembly at the outbreak of the French Revolution for the concession of civil rights to free mulattoes and for the emancipation of slaves in Haiti. Failing in his mission, he returned to Haiti in 1790 and, when the French governor refused to remove restrictions, headed an insurrection. Defeated, Ogé was tried, convicted of treason, and broken on the wheel.

4 LETTER TO LAVEAUX, 18 MAY 1794

1. On the complex historiographic debate surrounding Toussaint's *volte-face* to join the republican cause, see David Geggus, *Haitian Revolutionary Studies* (Indiana University Press, 2002), Chapter 8.

7 LETTER TO JEAN-FRANÇOIS, 13 JUNE 1795

1. Gérard M. Laurent, *Toussaint Louverture à travers sa correspondance (1794–1798)* (Madrid, 1953), p. 181.

8 LETTER TO DIEUDONNÉ, 12 FEBRUARY 1796

1. Toussaint also gave these couriers secret instructions to incite rebellion against Dieudonné should he fail to respond affirmatively to Toussaint's entreaty. This proved to be unnecessary, as Dieudonné's troops turned against their leader and joined Toussaint soon after.

13 LETTER TO THE FRENCH DIRECTORY, NOVEMBER 1797

1. For still-unsurpassed commentary on the world-historical nature of this letter, see C. L. R. James, *The Black Jacobins* (Vintage 1989 [1963]), pp. 194–8.

15 PROCLAMATION ON LABOUR, 1800

1. Archives nationales; colonies CC9B, 217 MIOM/12 (Déclarations de Toussaint).

18 ANTI-CORRUPTION PROCLAMATION, 9 THERMIDOR, YEAR 9 (29 JULY 1801)

1. Archives nationales; colonies CC9B, 217 MIOM/12 (Déclarations de Toussaint).

19 HAITIAN CONSTITUTION OF 1801

1. This world-historical constitution thus has the dubious distinction of having inaugurated the various totalitarian seizures of power and monopolizations of violence that would plague the decolonizing world a century and a half later, from Duvalier to Mobutu. For further analysis of this complex document, see Claude Moïse, *Le projet nationale de Toussaint Louverture et la constitution de 1801* (Port-au-Prince, 2001); Laurent Dubois, *Avengers of the New World* (Harvard University Press, 2004), pp. 242–6; Sibylle Fischer, *Modernity Disavowed: Haiti and the Cultures of Slavery in the Age*

of Revolution (Duke University Press, 2004); Madison Smartt Bell, *Toussaint Louverture: A Biography* (Pantheon, 2007), pp. 209–15; Nick Nesbitt, *Universal Emancipation: The Haitian Revolution and the Radical Enlightenment* (University of Virginia Press, 2008); Florence Gauthier, *Triomphe et mort du droit naturel en Révolution: 1789– 1795–1802* (PUF, 1992).

2. The formulation is radically innovative in the universal scope of its affirmation. Freedom from slavery constitutes the primary, onto-logical foundation of the society here envisaged; all subsequent qualifications and negations of freedom the document will go on to announce should thus be read in their contradiction to this founding premise.

3. This affirmation of a pure meritocracy sustains a fundamental innovation of post-1789 French republicanism.

4. The absolute equality of all before the law is one of the primary, unchanging imperatives of Toussaint's egalitarian politics. In its abstraction, of course, this fidelity says nothing about whether the particular laws to which all are to be equally subject are in fact just and emancipatory.

5. This intolerance of religious pluralism stands in stark contrast to the Enlightenment values of thinkers such as Spinoza and Locke. With this and subsequent clauses on marriage, morality and family, L'Ouverture definitively abandoned the Radical Enlightenment values that governed his emancipatory, anti-slavery politics in favour of the regressive, anti-Enlightenment conservatism of the Catholic Church and authoritarian nation-state. See Jonathan Israel, *Radical Enlightenment: Philosophy and the Making of Modernity, 1650–1750* (Oxford University Press, 2001).

6. This thirteenth clause is limited by the unconditional character of Article Three.

7. The essentialism of this formulation seeks to foreclose any possible debate on the nature of freedom in St-Domingue. Any competing vision of freedom (for example, the freedom to reappropriate one's surplus labour as labour-free time) will be silenced and expelled to the hinterland of the *moun endeyo* [the excluded] by the violence of L'Ouverture's authoritarian state apparatus. See Gérard Barthélemy, *L'Univers rural Haïtien: Le pays en dehors* (Harmattan, 1990).

8. The role of the metropolitan French government is not even mentioned in this definition of the legislative process; the

constitution envisages no more than an elective relation of consultation, a proposal verging on *de facto* independence. As Toussaint was well aware, this, combined with the document's immediate promulgation, was virtually guaranteed to provoke Napoleon into invading the island. The constitution nonetheless here invents, as Aimé Césaire observed, the concept of associated statehood.

9. Though such a stipulation was not uncommon in the period, this notorious clause inaugurates the sorry authoritarian tradition of the postcolonial ruler for life.

26 MEMOIR OF TOUSSAINT L'OUVERTURE

1. Cited in Laurent Dubois, *Avengers of the New World: The Story of the Haitian Revolution* (Harvard University Press, 2004), p. 255. See Madison Smartt Bell, *Toussaint Louverture: A Biography* (Pantheon, 2007), pp. 263–79; Daniel Desormeaux, 'The First of the (Black) Memorialists: Toussaint Louverture', in *Yale French Studies (The Haiti Issue)*, 107, pp. 131–45.

2. Toussaint had lived the majority of his life as a slave and, later, a free black on the Bréda Plantation, under its owner Bayon de Libertat. Before changing his name, he was known as Toussaint Bréda.

3. Toussaint finesses the fact that, until 1794, he had fought on the side of the Spanish against the French Republic.

4. As he consistently did throughout his career, Toussaint here invokes the rule of an abstract, universally applicable law to attack any discrimination based upon particularities of race or nation.

Printed in the United States
by Baker & Taylor Publisher Services